This book is a
Gift

To

_____

From

_____

On the occastion of

_____

Date

_____

You shall know the truth
and the truth shall
set you free
John 8:32

The Mystery of Sex

Understanding the Pleasures and Pains of Sex

by
Sam Kunle-Oluwatobi

Strategic Book Publishing and Rights Co.

Copyright © 2014 Samuel Kunle-Oluwatobi. All rights reserved.

No part of this book may be reproduced or transmitted in any form or by any means, graphic, electronic, or mechanical, including photocopying, recording, taping, or by any information storage retrieval system, without the permission, in writing, of the publisher.

Strategic Book Publishing and Rights Co.
12620 FM 1960, Suite A4-507
Houston, TX 77065

www.sbpra.com

ISBN: 978-1-61897-062-6

Design: Dedicated Book Services, (www.netdbs.com)

DEDICATION

This book is dedicated to my Lord and Savior, JESUS CHRIST, and to the woman whose intercessory prayers delivered me from the mouth of the lioness.

TABLE OF CONTENTS

Preface.................................viii
Acknowledgment...........................x
Chapter One: What is Sex? 1
Chapter Two: Man and His Consciousness......17
Chapter Three: God's Original Intention for Couples in Marriage......................40
Chapter Four: Sexual Intercourse in Marriage 59
Chapter Five: Your Marriage—The Soul of Your Life 107
Chapter Six: Common Sexual Perversions among Legally Married Couples............120
Chapter Seven: Your Virginity and Your Destiny 129
Chapter Eight: Spirit Husbands and Spirit Wives................................143
Chapter Nine: The Activities of Soul (Heart) Kidnappers..........................164
Chapter Ten: Sexual Attraction, Seduction, and Perversion 176

PREFACE

Sex is a gift of God to mankind. It is the foundation of life. This is why God detests sexual pollution and immorality in all forms.

However, man has unashamedly abused sex from generation to generation. The abuse, especially in this generation, calls for great concern and caution, as its evil impact on God's plans for man is getting worse by the day.

The Mystery of Sex is a revised edition of the previous publication titled The Mystery of Sexual Sin (Book 1). This edition provides deeper insight to various sexual perversions not only by the unmarried but also by the legally married couples.

Sex outside the divine purpose and plan can corrupt foundation of life, even of generations of children yet unborn. The corruptible sexual ties, which have viciously overtaken this generation, have brought great defilement upon the entire creation. The Bible says, *"The whole creation groans and travails in pain together until now" (Romans 8:22).*

Sexual pervasion leads to spiritual nakedness, dryness, and wantonness. They rob man of the glory and the perfect image of God in him and put him in the devil's bondage.

This book is inspired by God to bring deliverance to those who are already ensnared by the devil through sex.

I encourage you to read this book with all concentration. Meditate on it carefully. Pray the prayer points in it and consider how you relate with the opposite sex.

Samuel Kunle-Oluwatobi
Lagos, Nigeria.

ACKNOWLEDGMENT

I am very grateful to God for His special grace that made it possible for me to write this book.

I quite appreciate the contributions of the editorial team headed by Bro. Lekan Ojenike who read and edited the previous edition and the revised script.

Special thanks go to Messrs. Moses Akinkunmi, Pastor Areagbo, and Pastor Sayo Oluwaniyi for their encouragement.

I acknowledge the contributions of Prof. Olusola Oyewole of the University of Agriculture, Abeokuta, Nigeria, who read the very first manuscripts. He advised me to break the then manuscripts into two books. May God bless him greatly.

I must not fail to show my gratitude to Chief (Mrs.) Oluremi Tinubu, Mrs. F. C. Bah, and Engr. Rauf Aregbesola for their encouragement and assistance.

Lastly, I appreciate the efforts of Bro. Sunday Afagwu, Bro. Jide Akinteye, Edosa Oguigo, and others whose names are not mentioned because of space.

May God bless you all, in Jesus' mighty name.

Samuel Kunle-Oluwatobi
Lagos, Nigeria.

CHAPTER ONE
WHAT IS SEX?

Many people engage in sex as soon as they are of age—that is to say, when they begin to experience some biological changes in their body as they grow to adulthood. These changes naturally start in the teenage years. With these changes, there are some innate tendencies that attract males and females to each other.

This attraction is instinctive, a kind of magnetic pull. It makes males intensely desire their female counterparts, and vice-versa. This desire for each other often culminates in sex between a male and female. The urge for sex then can be said to be very powerful in man.

Sexual intercourse is the physical activity that describes the act of a man inserting his sexual organ into a woman's sexual organ.

Sexual intercourse is not a sin in itself. However, when it is performed outside divine order or precepts, it becomes sinful. This is a serious matter for a death sentence awaits all sexual sinners *(Leviticus 18:6-27).*

This conjugal relationship between male and female is essentially for procreation.

Newly born babies are not taught how to suck at their mother's breasts. God has created them to know the position of the breast, even when they are in their mother's arm. And a baby's ability to suck milk at his mother's breast is innate. Sex at adulthood is as naturally instructive.

> *Sex therefore is a phenomenon on which the procreation of mankind and continuity of human race revolves.*

DIFFERENT BIBLICAL DEFINITIONS OF SEXUAL INTERCOURSE

It is important to know certain facts about this mystery, sex, and have a proper understanding of what the Bible says about it in different situations.

In Genesis 4:1, the Bible says, *"And Adam knew Eve his wife; and she conceived and bore Cain."*

The word knew is used idiomatically to mean Adam had carnal knowledge of Eve. In other words, to know a woman is to have sex with her. Adam knew Eve, his wife. This statement is made in the context of marriage.

Let us consider other scriptures:

The Mystery of Sex

"Joseph a man espoused to Mary, the mother of our Lord Jesus Christ. She was found with a child of the Holy Ghost.

Then Joseph her husband being a just man, and not willing to make her a public example, was minded to put her away privately.

Having been warned by God through His Angel. Then Joseph being raised from sleep did as the angel of the Lord had bidden him and took to him his wife.

And know her not till she had brought forth her first born son and he called his name JESUS" (Matthew 1:8-25).

> A living man is the creation of God, and the life within him signifies the presence of God.

According to the Bible, in the context of legal marriage, having sex with one's wife is "knowing her."

Another way of expressing sexual intercourse in the context of marriage is "go in to her."

Jacob demanded from his prospective father-in-law and said to him, *"Give me my wife, for my days are fulfilled that I may go-in-to her"* (Genesis 29:21).

Jacob had served Laban for seven years for Rachael. All these seven years Jacob never made attempt to commit immorality with his would-be wife.

However, in the context of sexual immorality, the Bible has various idioms. The first idiom is "lie with." Lot's daughters decided to commit incest with their father by lying with him.

The father of these children was made to get drunk, and, under alcoholic influence, he committed grave immorality with his own daughters contrary to the commandment of God that says:

"*None of you shall approach to any that is near of kin to him to uncover their nakedness. I am the Lord*" *(Leviticus 18:6).*

> *Sex therefore, if done in sin, is a grave insult to the Almighty. It is an absolute disrespect to the Creator and all creations, even the entire universe.*

Lot's daughters uncovered the nakedness of their father and conceived and bore a son each to him.

The first daughter bore a son called Moab—who became the father of Moabites, and the second bore Benammi who became the father of Ammonites *(Genesis 19:32-38).*

These generations of Moabites and Ammonites, had a very faulty foundation, which was rooted in incest, a grave sin against God. The two generations became enemies of God and stood against everything God stands for. Their behavioral pattern often attracted curses from God and his prophets.

The wife of Potiphar, an officer of Pharaoh, who cast her eyes upon the young man, Joseph, actually approached Joseph and said, "Lie with me" *(Genesis 39:7).*

David, the King of Israel, arose from his bed one afternoon and walked upon the roof of the king's house,

The Mystery of Sex

and from the roof, he saw a woman washing herself; and the woman was very beautiful to look upon.

"And David sent messages and took her and she came in to him and he lay with her" (2 Samuel 11:2-4).

Amnon was sick for Tamar, his sister, and asked her to bring meat into his chamber that he, Amnon, may eat of her hand. And Amnon said, *"Come lie with me my sister" (2 Samuel 13:11).*

"And she answered him, No my brother, do not force me for no such thing ought to be done in Israel, do not you this folly" (2 Samuel 13:12).

"Howbeit, he would not hearken to her voice, but being stronger than her, she forced her and Lay with her" (2 Samuel 13:14).

> *Sexual Intercourse in man is supposed to be a way of union with God, a mode of worshipping God and an activity on which the existence and continuity of humans revolves.*

Hannah was married to Elkanah but bore no children for him; whereas Peninah, the second wife, had children for Elkanah.

And Hannah was in bitterness of soul and prayed to God and wept sore.

"After an encounter with Eli, the prophet of God, Eli said to her, 'Go in peace, and the God of Israel grant you your petition that you have asked of him.

"And the woman rose up in the morning early and worshipped before the Lord and returned and came to

their house in Ramah and El-Kanah knew Hannah his wife, and the Lord remembered her" (1 Samuel 1:17).

"Knowing one's wife" is in the context of legal marriage, which is recognized in heaven. But "lying with her" is in the context of sin, sexual immorality that leads to judgment of God and results in destruction.

THE BEGINNING OF CONJUGAL RELATIONSHIP BETWEEN MAN AND WOMAN

> *Sexual intercourse among animals therefore is for the fulfilment of their instinctive desires and for procreation.*

The beginning of conjugal relationship between men and women can be traced back to the book of Genesis where God decreed the fusion of man and his wife into one flesh. This fusion of man and his wife into one, body, soul, and spirit is the beginning of conjugal relationship that has its expression in sexual intercourse. It is through sexual intercourse that the will of God for man to cleave to his wife can be said to be operational.

"And the Lord God said it's not good that man should be alone, I will make him and help meet for him. And the Lord God caused a deep sleep to fall upon Adam and he slept, and took one of his ribs and closed the flesh instead thereof. And the ribs which the Lord God had taken from man made he a woman and brought her to the man. And Adam said, this is now the bone of my bone and the flesh of my flesh. She shall

The Mystery of Sex

be called woman (womb man) because she was taken out of man. Therefore shall a man leave his father and mother and shall cleave to his wife and they shall be one flesh." (Genesis 2:18-21).

Man is very central in all God's creations. God gave man dominion over everything He created. Aristotle, the great philosopher, described man as micro cosmos of all creations and existence. A living man is the creation of God, and the life within him signifies the presence of God. God is the custodian of life, and He (God) is the only Author of life. Therefore, whatever a man does while yet living, God beholds.

> *Sexual relationship between a man and an animal is regarded as confusion.*

God has given man a free will to choose whatsoever he desires. Man, however, has instructions from God to follow a particular pattern of life so that he can fulfill the program of God, as it is written of man even in heaven. Man therefore has the ability to obey God and follow, strictly, the instructions given to him by God so that he may enter the promise of God for his life. Conversely, man has the power to disobey God and follow the dictates of his heart. God did not create man as a robot without any inhibition or will power.

This is why one man behaves differently from another man. Every person in the world is distinct from others in thoughts, character, and way of life. God is present even in the thoughts of man. This is why man is different from animals.

"Death and Hell are opened to Him how much more the heart of men."

The Bible refers to the heart of man as *"deceitful above all things and desperately wicked. Who can know it?"* the Lord asked. Then said the Lord, *"I, the Lord search the heart, I try the reins, even to give every man according to his ways and according to the fruit of his doings"* (Jeremiah 17:9-10).

> Man however is not supposed to be ruled by fleshy desires or instincts, for he is a free moral agent.

Every activity of man is open to the Creator. Sexual activity, therefore, is a grave insult to the Almighty if done in sin. It is an absolute disrespect to the Creator. The seriousness of the matter lies in the fact that the consequences of this evil are not limited to the culprits but are also extended to the entire creations. This explains why God had to rain fire and brimstone upon the inhabitants of Sodom and Gomorrah.

Sexual intercourse among human beings is supposed to be a sign of union of a man and a woman, a mode of worship to God and an activity for procreation.

The Bible says God does not reside in a temple made with hands of men but in the temple of men made by God.

The Bible says, *"What? know you not that your body is the temple of the Holy Ghost which is in you which you have of God and you are not your own? You are bought with a price, therefore glorify God in your body and in your spirit which are God's (I Corinthians 6:19-20).*

This scripture is saying that man is living a borrowed life and that the life of man does not belong to Him. The body of man, the abode of God's, belongs to God. The soul of man within the three entities that make up man determines the character of man, the exercise of his will power and the consequences of his actions or inactions.

"The soul that sins shall die" (Ezekiel 18:46).

When a man commits any iniquity against the Lord with his body through sexual sin, he defiles his maker, the Creator, as the body belongs to the Creator, for it is written, *"The body is not for fornication but for the Lord and the Lord for the body. He that is joined with the Lord is in one spirit" (1 Corinthians 6:13).*

> *To fight and conquer the devil, the will of God must be done in totality. No place must be given to the devil.*

When a sister who is born again, sanctified, and filled with the Holy Ghost is joined in holy matrimony to a brother who is also born again, sanctified, and filled with the Holy Ghost, the two become one body. By extension, they are united in the Lord. That is to say, they are married to Christ.

They are in one union in Christ. If they remain faithful to their God till the end of the age, Christ shall take them home, and they shall be united for ever with the Lord, married to the Lamb of God eternally. Holy marriage here on earth is a symbol of eternal marriage with the Lamb of God.

Sexual intercourse in man means so much to the Almighty and to the entire creation. This is why it is allowed only in marriage. It is the exclusive right of those who are legally married.

SEXUAL INTERCOURSE AMONG ANIMALS

God created or formed animals out of the ground. *"All the beasts of the field were formed from the dust" (Genesis 2:19).*

> *Sexual intercourse is the greatest and most effective weapon of the devil to bring man into destruction against the will of God.*

However, man was made in the image of God. God, the Almighty, has a moral nature. Man who was made in the image of God too has a moral nature. He is also a free moral agent. This moral nature of God and man does not exist in animals. This is why man is higher in nature than the wild beasts of the earth. Man is given power and dominion over everything God created. Therefore, man can tame the wildest beast to conform to his dictates.

Animals do not have a moral nature. They don't have communion with God or ability to worship Him consciously. However, they still declare His glory. They lack moral standards, so they are ruled by their instincts, pushed by their immediate desire.

Sexual intercourse among animals is for the fulfillment of their instinctive desires, and for procreation. They lack moral inhibition. When they desire it, they go for it. This is why dogs can go on mating in an open field without any inhibition, likewise other animals. However, there are some who will not mate in the open. Sometimes they operate in an exclusive way. The reason for this is that each animal operates with its kind, patterned according to God's will.

One thing is sure about animals: their ways are strictly what God created them to be; they don't have free will outside God's will. If there is any strange behavior in any animals, it is because everything God has created is liable to corruption. Man, through satanic influences, can control animals outside God's will.

> *Many destinies have been terminated on the altar of illicit sexual games.*

The devil has turned the whole world into wilderness and subjected the creation to corruption and pollution. Even serpent was not created for the devil. The devil just entered into the serpent and began to work through it for evil purposes. Sometimes man, through the influence of Satan, works evil through animals and beasts. The Bible says, *"They changed their glory into the similitude of an ox that eats grass" (Psalm 106:20).*

Why did they do this? It is because they forget their God, their Savior who had done great things for them.

It is not strange to hear that human beings sleep with animals. Some women do have sex with dogs while some men have sex with strange animals. This situation occurs under intense satanic influences. Whosoever has done that has changed his glory into the similitude of an ox that eats grass. It is a serious demotion from the image of God to the similitude of animals. Sexual relationship between man and animals is regarded as confusion. *"Neither shall they lie with any beast to defile yourself therewith, neither shall any woman stand before a beast to lie thereto. It is confusion" (Leviticus 18:23).*

Animals operate only in God's will. A goat will not go and mate with a dog. Never! It is the man under evil influences that does things that are contrary to the will of God. But man is not supposed to be ruled by fleshy desires or instincts; for he is a free moral agent. Animals, however, are ruled by their natural instincts and immediate desires.

WHY GOD CREATED MAN

And God said, *Let us make man in our image, after our likeness and let them have dominion over the fish of the sea, and over the fowl of the air, and the cattle, and over all the earth and over every creeping thing that creeps upon the earth. So God created man in his own image*

The Mystery of Sex

and in the image of God created him, male and female created he them.

And God blessed them and God said to them, be fruitful and multiply and replenish the earth, and subdue it and have dominion over the fish of the sea, and over the fowl of the air, and over every living thing that moves upon the Earth (Genesis 1:26-28).

God the father of Glory had to call a conference to decide the creation of man. "Let us make man in our image . . ." God Himself is a self-sufficient and self-sustaining eternal God. God created man in His image for man to manifest His glory on the surface of the earth and to manifest as His son.

"The earnest expectation of the creature waits for manifestation of the sons of God" (Romans 8:19).

Man is supposed to act as God on the surface of the earth, to enforce God's Will upon the rebellious—that the will of God must be done here on earth as it is in heaven.

> **Judgement against Satan and sin is already set and settled. No second chance.**

God created man to show forth His glory, to worship Him in holiness, in righteousness, and to deliver the entire creation from the bondage of corruption into the glorious liberty of the children of God" *(Romans 8:12).*

Since the great dragon and his demons were cast down from heaven, following a failed fierce battle with Michael, their place is no more found in heaven. The great dragon, having been cast out onto the earth, has converted the whole earth into wilderness; brought woe to all the inhabitants of the earth and of the sea, and determined to destroy the entire world. God therefore created man to confront and conquer the devil, who has put the whole world in the bondage of corruption.

This is why immediately after the first Adam failed, God had to send down the second Adam from heaven to destroy the operation of the enemy of God. The second Adam was Jesus Christ who came in the likeness of man to deliver the whole world from bondage of sin and corruption.

To fight and conquer the devil, the will of God must be done in totality. No place must be given to the devil.

The Bible refers to the devil as the old man, the prince of this world, the adversary, the enemy of God, accuser of brethren, the tempter who has come to kill, to steal, and to destroy. His agenda for man is to take away the place of God in their lives so as to lead man into everlasting destruction.

The strategy of the devil to achieve these goals is to lead man away from God: to deceive them out of God's program, to influence them to rebel against God, to lead them into sin against God.

Sexual sin is the greatest and the most effective weapon of the devil to bring man to destruction, against the will of God.

> *When a soul now commits sexual sins, he moves over to be in union with Satan the author of sin.*

The Mystery of Sex

The program of God for Joseph in the Land of Egypt was to become the prime minister in that land, so as to preserve meat for his brethren during the period of famine.

Joseph found himself in the home of his master, Potiphar, an officer of Pharaoh and captain of the guard. This master saw that the Lord was with him and that the Lord made all that he did to prosper in his hand. He therefore made him the overseer over his house and over all that he had. And the Lord blessed the Egyptian's house for Joseph's sake. Satan knew that Joseph was on his way to achieve the purpose of God for his life in the land of Egypt. And to destroy that purpose, the wife of Potiphar his master, under satanic influence, offered him free sex.

"And his master's wife cast her eyes upon him, upon Joseph; and she said, 'Lie with me'" (Genesis 39:7).

However, Joseph refused that satanic offer, saying, *"Behold, my master knows not what is with me in the house, and he has committed all that he has to my hand. And there is none greater in this house than I, neither has he kept back anything from me but you, because you are his wife: how then can I do this great wickedness and sin against God?* (Genesis 39:8-9).

> The conscience is that discovery which distinguishes between right and wrong; between good and evil or bad.

Joseph regarded sexual sin as great wickedness and sin against God. He, therefore, did not hearken to her, to lie by her, or to be with her. She then became furious and set Joseph up. Eventually, Joseph was thrown into the prison, a place of destiny from where he became the prime minister of the land.

Had Joseph consented to that sexual offer, it would have been the end of his destiny.

Spiritually, that woman could have terminated the destiny of the young man, Joseph, in the land of Egypt. A lot of destinies have been terminated on the altar of illicit sexual game.

Many people who are supposed to rule over their environment have been converted to doormats on the altar of sex. Sex is an effective weapon of destruction, especially in these last days. God created man for a definite purpose, to fulfill a divine agenda. The original intention of God for bringing a man to this world is his destiny. This can be terminated permanently through illicit sexual relationship.

CHAPTER TWO
MAN AND HIS CONSCIOUSNESS

THE NATURAL MAN

Man is the most outstanding of God's creatures: he is made in the image of God and is the replica of God. However, he has become, albeit ignorantly, the opposite of God's original intention for man. He has, over the years, become an expert through the knowledge God gave to him for studying the operations of other creatures in his environment: the operation of plants and animals in the physical and climatic environments. Man has also become knowledgeable by studying the physical nature of man and neglecting the spiritual state that is God's nature in man.

The Bible says, *God is a Spirit and those that worship Him must do so in spirit and in truth (John 4:24)*. If God is a Spirit, man, being an image of God, is also a spirit. However, man has forgotten his relationship with God, his Creator. The natural man now lives under the control of his flesh, his brain, and his limited understanding, as sin has taken absolute control of him.

Adam, the first man to be created, found himself naked after he disobeyed God, his Maker. He was separated from God and died spiritually. The glory and perfect image of God in him left him, and he became naked.

The devil who influenced man to disobey God then took advantage of his nakedness and brought about his sinful nature upon man instead of the righteousness of God, which was originally God's intention for man. Rather than man to operate in the righteousness of God, he now operates in the sinful nature of Satan. *Therefore, man has come short of the glory of God (Romans 3:23).*

> *Anyone who is sexually loose stands the greatest risk of being manipulated into making the worst decision of his life which may result in everlasting sorrow.*

This sinful nature of Satan is highly operated in three principal areas: the lust of the eyes, the lust of flesh, and the pride of life. All these three attributes lead to eternal separation from God, which is destruction.

Judgment against Satan and sin is already set, and it is settled. No second chance. But man still has another opportunity to reconcile with God. This can be done by experiencing a new birth. That is to say, to have a spiritual rebirth.

Anyone who still lives according to the dictates of his mind and flesh is automatically under the influence of the prince of the air, the spirit that rules in the midst of children of disobedience *(Ephesians 2:2).*

The natural man is a composition of body, soul, and spirit; however, the spiritual aspect is dead. That is to say, the natural man is not conscious of the existence of the living God. God had departed from him with His Glory.

Anyone who is still operating as a natural man is ruled by his flesh and by the dictates of his mind.

THE SPIRITUAL MAN

Man, as noted earlier, is a composition of body, soul and spirit.

BODY

This is the vessel that holds both the soul and the spirit. It determines the consciousness of the world around us.

> *Any form of sexual sin will bring defilement not only to the body, but also to the soul and the spirit.*

SOUL

This is the consciousness of self, the character, and the unique personal identity.

SPIRIT

This is the inner man that constitutes the spiritual personality. And this is where the nature of God and the consciousness of the living God resides.

They that are led by the spirit of God, are called the children of God" (Romans 8:14). "To be carnally minded is death, but to be spiritually minded is life and peace"

(Romans 8:6). "They that are in the flesh cannot please God. But you are not in the flesh, but in the spirit, if the spirit of God dwells in you or if any man has not the spirit of Christ, he is none of his. And if Christ be in you, the body is dead because of sin, but the spirit is life because of righteousness" (Romans 8:8-10).

THE SPIRIT OF MAN

The spirit of man has three functions or three basic departments (1) Realm of soul or conscience, (2) intuition, (3) communion with God.

1. CONSCIENCE

> *It is discovered that land can be defiled through sexual sin; and, in fact, families and nations can also be defiled and be sold to Satan through sexual immorality.*

The conscience is that discovery that distinguishes between right and wrong, between good and evil or bad. That thing inside you that tells you that what you have just done is bad. It is the police that is living inside everyman, even every soul. Its operation is instant and spontaneous, and it is very independent. It has no respect for you or your opinion. It is the voice of accusation *(Psalm 51:10).*

2. INTUITION

This is the sensing organ of human spirit. It is the complete opposite of other five senses: seeing, hearing, tasting, feeling, and touching. This is the knowledge that comes to us without thinking about it. It is the knowledge that comes from above. It is the information you have without thinking about it. If anyone can develop that sense, it will prevent him a lot from entering into problems. If you pray for directions from God, and listen, you will know what to do, but you may not be able to explain how you get the directions. This is intuition.

3. THE COMMUNION

This is the ability to worship God in spirit and in truth. Whether a man will perish or not, the spirit is not destructive. It is either in union with God or in union with Satan.

When a soul commits sexual sins, he is in union with Satan, the author of sins.

THE SOUL OF MAN

The soul of man is that aspect that makes a man conscious of himself. Sometimes, one can be respectful, harsh, or stubborn. It makes different behavioral patterns. It is the seat of man's personality.

All the immoralities going on in our environment might be the cause of the troubles around us.

It is responsible for our intellect, emotion, choices, and decisions. The soul of man determines a man's personality, the willpower, and ability to choose. It determines his thoughts, imaginations, hope and ideals. The soul of man has three principal departments (i) The mind, (ii) volition, and (iii) the emotion.

i. The Mind

The mind determines our thoughts, imaginations, hopes, and ideals.

The mind, being the organ of thoughts, is so important that it is the area of struggle between the Spirits of God and Satan.

Before the new birth, evil spirit walks into the mind of man freely without his consent. The way evil spirit has built strongholds in the minds of many.

> *A lot of people have acquired curses, poverty, sickness, and infirmities, etc. through sex*

When the devil came to tempt Jesus Christ in the wilderness, he spoke to his mind. *If you are the son of God, command these stones be made bread (Matthew 4:3).*

All the temptations went on in the mind of Christ.

Man's intelligence can hinder him from understanding God or help him to understand God. Many minds have been blinded by the devil. However, God can reach out through his mercy, and man would have a change of mind. It is you, not God, who will face the battle in your mind. What are those things that go on in your mind?

Who is in control of your mind, your thoughts? Is it the Holy Spirit or the devil? To win constant battle of the mind, the word of God is needed to checkmate Satan and his hosts. Jesus used the word of God.

Many people are committing immoralities every day, especially in their minds. You must ensure perfect control of what enters into your mind. Eject them

The Mystery of Sex

instantly when you discover them to be outside God's words.

Finally brethren whatsoever things are true, whatsoever things are honest, whatsoever things are just, whatsoever things are pure, whatsoever things are lovely, whatsoever things are of good report; if there be any virtue, and if there be any praise, think on these things (Philippians 4:8).

Anything outside the Bible's recommendations should not be allowed even for a second in your mind. Sexual sins start from the mind. We must therefore always guide against sins by not making our mind blank. The blank mind is an invitation to the devil and is often occupied by the evil spirits. The duty of man is to love God with all his heart and mind and love his neighbor as himself. There must be constant renewal of our minds with the word of God.

> *Many people died and many have received a death sentence on the altar for a few minutes of sexual pleasure.*

ii. THE VOLITION

The volition is the right of decision. It gives the power to choose. When a man is without volition, he's reduced to a robot or puppet. It is the willpower. When you choose well, then you are happy. It manifests our intellectual power. It is the ability to think and choose between good and bad. It is this aspect of man that Satan loves to manipulate.

Many people have been captured through satanic influence: Many have married wrong wives and wrong husbands.

Anyone who is sexually loose stands the greatest risk of being manipulated into taking the worst decision of his life. And this may even result in everlasting sorrow.

Today, many people reject Jesus Christ because their volition is influenced by the devil.

> *Sexual sins can lead to spiritual repositioning. ... You should therefore not indulge in sex like beasts devoid of understanding. It has its attendant spiritual implications.*

iii. THE EMOTION

This plays a very big role in the life of man. It can be divided into three parts: affection, desires, and feelings.

a. AFFECTION

The Lord God requires every child of his to submit his affection to him. "You shall love the Lord your God with all your heart, your soul and your mind." God must be loved in all circumstances.

Our affection must be checked from time to time. Ask yourself, "Am I seeking the glory of God or the glory of man or the glory of the opposite sex?'

b. DESIRES

Desires are ambition. These must also be checked constantly. It is self-delight or self-importance. One must be careful lest personal desires leads to way of pride. Our motive for doing certain things must be checked, Else silent pride can easily creep into one's life. Our principal desire must be to satisfy God, our Creator.

The Mystery of Sex

It is sometimes very difficult to appreciate how these desires can affect our lives. One needs to wait on the Lord. Wait for His time and learn to be patient and to exercise self-control. Many people always justify themselves for their wrongs, even when the motives behind their actions revolve around self-desires.

c. Feelings

God gives us joy when we come to Him. We sometimes enter into His presence effortlessly but have to make efforts at some other time. Sometimes when we are happy, we have right feelings. But when we are sad, there is heaviness in our heart. Whatever the problems are, our God is the same; He does not change.

> *Sexual intercourse brings transference of spirits between the partners involved.*

Sexual Intercourse as it Affects the Totality of Man

Time has been taken to analyze man in his relationship with God. Any form of sexual sin would bring defilement not only to the body but also to the soul and the spirit. And when a man is defiled, all his totality is presumed defiled, even the seeds of his body, his children, and children's children. Unfortunately, the land in which he is dwelling is presumed defiled also. And when the land is defiled all that dwell on that land, by extension, are defiled also. Let us check out the following scriptures.

"*Defile not you yourselves in any of these things: for in all these the nations are defiled which I cast out before you: And the land is defiled: therefore I do visit the iniquity thereof upon it, and the land vomits out her inhabitants.*

"*You shall therefore keep my statues and my judgements, and shall not commit any of these abominations: neither any of your own nation nor any stranger that sojourns among you. For all these, abominations have the men of the land done, which were before you, and the land is defiled*" *(Leviticus 18:24-27).*

> God made coats of skin to cover their nakedness. The only activity that can uncover this covered nakedness is sexual intercourse.

"*Woe to the bloody city! it is all full of lies and robbery; the prey departeth not: The noise of a whip, and the noise of the rattling of the wheels, and of the prancing horses, and of the jumping chariots. The horseman lifts up both the bright sword and the glittering spear; and there is a multitude of slain, and great number of carcases; and there is non end of their corpses; they stumble upon their corpses. Why?*

"*Because of the multitude of the whoredoms of the well favored harlot, the mistress of witchcrafts that sells nations through her whoredom and families through her witchcrafts*". *(Nahum 3:1-3).*

In considering these two scriptures, I discover that land can be defiled through sexual sins, and families and nations can also be defiled and sold to Satan through sexual immoralities. Unfortunately, leaders in high places, rulers of nations, do not understand this. And there are lots of immoral (sexual) sins going on in the high places.

Where this is common in any nation or country, there will be poverty, robbery, untimely death, chaos, and wars or any form of evil work, which evil spirits consequently unleash upon the inhabitants. All the immoralities going on in our environment might be the cause of the troubles around us.

Nations that understand this stand against such immoralities, even among their leaders. When an individual commits a sexual sin, his body, soul, and spirit are involved. The seeds of his body that would produce his generation are involved. It brings a negative multiplier effect upon his generation and the land.

> *The phrase 'uncover their nakedness', or 'uncover her nakedness' means 'have sex with them or her', as the case may be. To have sex with someone means to uncover the nakedness of that fellow.*

SPIRITUAL IMPLICATION OF SEXUAL SIN

When a man or a woman falls into sexual sin, the totality of that man or woman, or both of them who commit that sin, is brought under the judgment of God. And a legal ground would be given to the devil to take over the affairs of their lives and destinies.

Their totality shall be brought under defilement. The Bible says the two shall come together and they shall be one flesh. This scripture is saying that the two that have sex together are in one union with each other. This means their spiritual compositions are now in one union with themselves. For example, if a child of God who is born clean into a family, household of faith, and sanctified, falls into sexual sins with a witch whose foundation is an idol worshipping, that child of God automatically becomes one union with a witch.

Ahab was a king in Israel. He entered into a marriage relationship with Jezebel, the daughter of Ethbaal. And Jezebel made Ahab to forsake the God of his fathers. She turned the heart of her husband to the idols of her father's house. Ahab then raised altar to Baal and forsook the God of Israel.

How was Jezebel able to turn away the heart of her husband? It was through sexual intercourse. It suffices to say, immediately they became one flesh, Ahab was in union with evil and idolatry, which oppose God in all ways. He had been yoked together with a personality that pursued and promoted agenda that oppose God. Ahab then became blind to the existence of God of Israel on whose throne he sat.

> *The consequences of sexual sins are enormous and grave. They bring instant judgement and disaster from God and also from Satan upon the disobedient. Sexual sins bring evil consumption upon the body.*

The Bible says *"Be you not unequally yoked together with unbelievers: for what fellowship has righteousness*

The Mystery of Sex

with unrighteousness, and what communion has light with darkness. And what concord has Christ with belial?" (2 Corinthians 6:14-15).

Samson was warned by his parents not to get married to the uncircumcised Philistine but he rejected his parents' advice and ended up in tragedy (Judges 14:3).

Sexual intercourse has a very deep spiritual blood covenant. It brings the couple into a serious and very deep spiritual union. It mixes their blood together. So whatsoever each of them stood for before the act, they both share with each other after the act. A lot of people have acquired curses, poverty, sickness and infirmities, et cetera, through sexual intercourse.

SEX LEADS TO SPIRITUAL REPOSITIONING

"King Solomon loved many strange women together with the daughter of Pharaoh, women of the Moabites, Ammorites, Edomites, Zidonians and Hittites of the nations concerning which the Lord said to the children of Israel. You shall not go in to them [have sex with them] neither shall they come in [have sex with you] for surely they will turn away your heart after their gods. Solomon clave to these in love" (I Kings 11:1-2).

> *So, boys and girls who engage in sexual activities are digging their graves.*

King Solomon was formerly on the side of God, but when he began to lust after strange women whom he cleaved to, his heart turned away from God. Through sexual intercourse, one can automatically cross over from righteousness to unrighteousness and from the Kingdom God to the Kingdom of darkness. Many careless men of God have lost their positions with God for falling into sexual sin.

Sexual sin can lead to a serious spiritual repositioning, from life to eternal destruction. You should therefore not indulge in it like beasts devoid of understanding. It has its attendant spiritual implications.

SPIRITUAL MATHEMATICS OF SEXUAL INTERCOURSE

When two people engage in sexual activities, some personalities will be indirectly involved. The number of these personalities is determined by the previous sexual experience of each of the couple. For example, when a young man who has never had sex mates with a woman who has previously had it with two different men, the spirits of the two men that must have entered the woman during coitus, together with the woman's spirits, will enter the man.

> *When two children of God, male and female, come together in holy matrimony, the ultimate aim is to bring children into existence.*

Sexual intercourse causes transference of spirit beings between the partners involved.

When a harlot sleeps with a playboy Casanova, they run the risk of transferring a minimum of six thousand demons or demonic spirits to each other.

The six thousands personalities, which are called Legion in the Bible, are the minimum. One can imagine sleeping with a woman or harlot who has lost count of the number of men she has ever slept with.

There are some satanic agents who target a minimum of one thousand men within a stipulated period of time. These satanic agents are soul traders who trade in souls of men to Satan. And they capture the souls through sex.

Let us consider the origin of this in the scriptures. In Genesis 3, Adam and Eve fell into the sin of disobedience. The Bible says, *"The eyes of them both were opened and they knew that they were naked and they sew fig leaves together and made themselves aprons" (Genesis 3:7).*

Before then, Adam and Eve were covered with the glory of God, having been created in the image of God. But immediately they fell into sin, that nature of God, which is His glory and His righteousness, departed from them. Then they became naked. And the nature of God and his glory in them were replaced with nakedness, shame, and sin, the nature of Satan who deceived them into disobedience against God.

Experience from counselling has shown that many problems are brought to the family through illicit sexual games.

Consequent upon their disobedience to God, God cursed them and the land on which they treaded. When a man sins, the land on which he treads is cursed.

Toward the end of chapter three of Genesis, the Lord God had to send them out of the beautiful Garden of

Eden, lest they put forth their hands on the tree of life and live forever as sinners. God had to give them another opportunity to allow the nature of sin, which they acquired through disobedience, to die so that they would reconcile with God and their spirit would conform again to the nature of God.

God in His mercy did not send them away naked. In verse 21 of chapter three, God made coats of skin and clothed them before sending them out of Eden.

A deep understanding of that verse reveals the fact that God shed blood of an animal for the sin they committed. "God made coats of skin to cover their nakedness." The only activity that can uncover this covered nakedness is sexual intercourse.

> It should be known that sexual acts in the presence of children can be very disastrous for the marriage and even the children.

The Bible says, *"None of you shall approach to any that is of kin to him to uncover their nakedness; I am the Lord. The nakedness of your father or the nakedness of your mother shall you not uncover. She is your mother; you shall not uncover her nakedness"* (Leviticus 18:6).

The phrase "uncover their nakedness" or "uncover her nakedness" refers to sex. To have sex with someone means to uncover the nakedness of that fellow and vice-versa. When nakedness of someone is uncovered by a stranger, all good things that God created in the person's life and covered with coats of skin could be stolen.

The Mystery of Sex

When those good things are stolen, bad things will replace them, for the Bible says, *"Let their habitation be desolate and their place let another take" (Psalm 69:25).* Satan too uses the word of God against the children of God who fall into sin.

The devil is referred to as "a thief who has come to steal, to kill and to destroy." The greatest means of carrying out these threefold agenda is the power of sexual intercourse.

When a man or woman falls into sexual sin, all the good things in his or her life—such as the spirit of prosperity, favor of God and man, spirit of dominion over God's creature, the grace to multiply and to replenish the earth, spirits or power to grow in the Lord and His might, power of faith, helmet of salvation, sword of the spirit, and all other good things that make life meaningful—are promptly stolen and replaced with spirits of poverty, nakedness, filthiness, barrenness, sickness, infirmities, anger, lying, as many as Satan and his agents could release into that life.

> *Christian couples must ensure that they treat sex as secret and sacred. They must also have an assurance of the presence of God Almighty.*

A lot of lives and destinies can be ruined on account of sin. Such lives, however, are not afflicted only by Satan; God approves the affliction and supervises it.

Sexual sins cause defilement of the temple of God. And whosoever destroys the temple of God, God shall destroy.

If one considers the words of God in *Deuteronomy 28:22, 27, 35* one will clearly see the manifestations or the symptom of HIV/AIDS which is consuming the human race now.

"The Lord shall smite you with a consumption, and with a fever and with an inflammation, and with an extreme burning and with the sword, and with blasting, and with mildew, and until you perish. . . . The Lord will smite you with the botch of Egypt, and with the emerods, and with the scabs, and with the itch of which you cannot be healed. . . . The Lord shall smite you in the knees and in the legs with a sore botch that cannot be healed, from the sole of your foot to the top of your head."

> *The relationship between God and married couples must be taken with utmost care and meticulous seriousness.*

Beloved, check out the symptoms of HIV and AIDS. They are all loaded in this scriptural passage. It is important to read *Deuteronomy 28* from the beginning to the end.

The consequences of sexual sin are enormous and grave. Sexual sin brings instant judgment and disaster from God and also from Satan for the disobedient. It brings evil consumption upon the body.

The Bible says, *"Flee fornication, every sin that a man does is without the body; but he that committeth fornication sins against his own body"* (1 Corinthians 6:18). The Bible further says, *"If you cannot contain, let them marry for it is better to marry than to burn!"* (1 Corinthians 7:9).

Sexual intercourse is allowed only in marriage. So boys and girls who engage in sex are digging their graves. It has grave consequences. When anyone commits sexual sins, he defiles his body, soul, and spirit and God, who is the owner of the body. As a result, he invites the devil into his life, and evil spirits will destroy the precious life, which is meant to be lived only once.

SEX AS A MEANS OF PROCREATION

"God created man in His own image. In the image of God created He him, male and female created he them. And God blessed them and God said to them be fruitful and multiply, and replenish the Earth" (Genesis 1:27-28).

The blessing pronounced upon Adam and Eve at the beginning of creation is still working effectively. God will not come down again to mold any man. The Power to be fruitful and multiply He has given to man.

Man and his wife are mandated to procreate their kind and replenish the earth. The agenda of God is to bring all his sons into his Glorious kingdom. Man is made a partaker of God's creation.

"For we are labourers together with God; you are God's husbandry, you are God's building" (1 Corinthians 3:9).

This scripture is saying we are fellow workmen—joint promoters, laborers together, co-creators, co-makers with God and for God. Man is God's garden and vineyard and field under cultivation. Man is God's building.

When two children of God, male and female, come together in holy matrimony, the ultimate aim is to bring children into existence.

Sex in marriage, therefore, is a role assigned to man that enables him to partake in God's agenda of creation. This means when a husband and wife come together in bed, God is there with them. They are not alone. Any form of sexual misadventure by the couple could provoke the anger of God against them, which may have a negative consequence upon the child born into that marriage.

A young man traveled to America. For many years, he could not achieve anything. Nothing ever worked for him. He tried so many things; nothing worked for him. He then gave his life to Christ and started praying. One night, after his prayer, he was taken out in the spirit and saw a vision. He saw two people, a man and a woman, having sex, standing. At a close look, he observed these people were his parents. At a closer look, he saw an Angel of God, furious and pointing a sword to the mating couple. The angel told him "it was in this situation that you were conceived. And that is the cause of your problem in life." Then the vision cleared. When the man woke up, he broke down in tears and prayed in repentance on behalf of his late parents.

> *Fellowship of married couples with God is fundamental to their living, both in this present world and that which is to come.*

Through sexual misadventures, the foundation of life can be destroyed.

"If the foundation be destroyed, what can the righteous do" (Psalm 11:3).

The Mystery of Sex

Many married couples, even born again Christians who claim to be sanctified and spirit filled, do, as a matter of fact, engage in various forms of sexual misadventures or malpractices that range from pornography, oral sex, and some other forms of perversion. They justify such malpractices, claiming that they don't do them outside marriage.

My experience in counseling shows that many problems are brought to the family through illicit sexual acts.

Illicit sexual acts greatly undermine the presence of God in your home and provide legal grounds to the devil to operate against you and your children.

If the Lord has an agenda for a particular family to bear a child who is to carry out a specific assignment for Him, and such a couple engage in an illicit sexual act, God may render them childless. Barrenness is very common in Christian homes. And Satan launches his attack on Christian marriages more than he does on unbelievers. Christians must be aware of this reality and watch out and guide against any satanic influence. If others do wrong things, such iniquities must not be named among you the children of Most High God.

> *Fellowship of married couples with God is fundamental to their living, both in this present world and hereafter.*

SEX MUST BE SECRET AND SACRED

As I have said earlier, God is with godly married couples when they mate. Apart from God, no personality is expected to witness this act between husband and wife.

To ensure the secrecy and sacredness of sex, Christian couples must worship God and pray for His presence before they start. They need to be enveloped with the fire of God to prevent the prying eyes of personalities who may want to watch them in the act for pleasure and evil. It is not good to allow the devil and his agents to watch the act of lovemaking between husband and wife. The presence of the devil and his agents brings nothing good, but woes, anguish and sorrow.

Some satanic mothers-in-law travel in the spirit, every night, into their sons' bedroom with witchcraft calabash, which they use to collect the semen of their sons. They do this to make conception impossible for their daughters-in-law. The women are then childless not knowing that some evil people are standing in their way of conception. Sometimes the evil mothers-in-law can allow conception, but they weaken the women's womb, to prevent them from carrying the pregnancy to full term. In such a situation, what results most often is miscarriage or still birth.

Worse still, enemies do plant strange children in various homes. Once such children are born into a family they do not allow another child to come into that marriage. So when couples with strange children make love in the presence of such children, they worsen the problem(s) confronting them in their marriage.

It should be known that lovemaking in the presence of children can be very damaging to the marriage, and even to the children. This is because it allows certain evil spirits to enter into the children. Parents must be aware of this and guide against it.

If poverty has limited a couple with grown-up children to one room, such a couple must pray themselves out of poverty to be able to afford a bigger apartment.

Christian couples must ensure that they treat sex as secret and sacred. They must also have an assurance of the presence of God Almighty when they mate. Aggressive worship and prayers are important before lovemaking if you must fulfill God's agenda for your home. Allow the Spirit of God inside you to rule over your canal lust, emotion, and desires. Also exercise a great deal of restraint in your bedroom.

CHAPTER THREE

GOD'S ORIGINAL INTENTION FOR COUPLES IN MARRIAGE

God said "It is not good that a man should be alone. I will make him an help meet for him" (Genesis 2:18).

God created man and was having fellowship with him in the garden of Eden at the cool of the day. Then God felt it was not good enough for the man to be alone. He too needed fellowship—a companion and helper. God therefore made him a suitable helper with whom to live in love and in fellowship.

The original intention of God for marriage institution is fellowship. Couples who have fellowship with God exemplify the truth of God concerning his love for mankind.

The presence of a suitable companion in marriage symbolizes the pleasure that can be derived even in the presence of God.

God is our Maker. He's always with us, for he has promised not to leave us alone. He understands the evil of loneliness and its attendant insecurity, vis-à-vis the operation of the roaring lion seeking whom to devour *(1 Peter 5:8)*.

There is always a ready-made assistance for a child of God. This is why Jesus told His disciples before He departed to heaven, *"Lo I am with you always even to the end of the world" (Matthew 28:20)*.

God instituted marriage originally for companionship and fellowship. In the physical realm, a man and woman in marriage are supposed to be united both physically and spiritually. They must agree with each other in all things that must not be contrary to the will of God.

They must also recognize that the presence of their Creator is forever with them and that they must not do anything to mar their relationship with Him. They should recognize that God enjoys their fellowship, worship, and open declaration of His Glory in their union. As God's Saints, their worship brings a sweet savor and acceptable daily sacrifice to God's presence. The worship must be a daily affair, for it will be recorded in their favor and earn them a permanent place at God's right hand in heaven. Therefore, married couples must be serious in their relationship with God. They must avoid anything that will adversely affect their relationship with Him.

> *The husband's body has been given to the wife, while that of the wife has been pledged to the husband.*

Their body must be presented before God as a living sacrifice, holy (since God is holy) and acceptable to God, which is a reasonable service demanded from them. They must not conform to the dictates of the perishing world but continually have renewal of their minds through the word of God. They must consistently prove what is good and acceptable, perfect will of God *(Romans 12:1-21)*. They must always hope for that glorious declaration: "This is my beloved child, in whom I am well pleased."

Fellowship of married couples with God is fundamental to their living both in this present world and that which is to come. Marriage in the Lord must *"be made honourable in all and the bed undefiled" (Hebrews 13:4)*.

The judgment of God surely awaits all whoremongers and adulterers.

> *The fallen nature of man is manifested through lust after sin; and sin leads to death.*

"It is a fearful thing to fall into the hands of the living God" (Hebrews 11:31).

SEX AS A MODE OF WORSHIP

Sexual intercourse in holy marriage can also be a form of worship to the Almighty God. Therefore, it must be done with reverence to God by husbands and wives. Couples must conform to this precept of holiness, recognizing the fact that their bodies are the temple of the living God, and that the same God must be glorified in their bodies *(1 Corinthians 6:20)*. Then they will be dear to God.

The Mystery of Sex

The Bible says, *"I will dwell in them and walk in them and I will be their God and they shall be my people. And I will be a father to you and you shall be my sons and daughters, said the Lord Almighty" (2 Corinthians 16:18)*.

As soon as a man and woman are together in bed, an altar is raised either to God or to the devil.

What is an altar? An altar is the place where man and spirit beings meet. An altar is a place of worship. An altar is a place of sacrifice. An altar is a place of slaughter.

Now for the purpose of our discourse, sexual intercourse between man and woman could mean raising up an altar to the Lord or to the devil.

> *It has to be noted, that lust is not love.*

If it is done in marriage and with reverence to the Lord, honorable and without defilement of the bed, the Lord's presence would be felt. On the contrary, if it is done in sin, an altar is automatically raised to the devil and his agents. They too will operate and their presence will manifest.

However, the presence of the devil will not bring forth anything good. It is important to say this for God promised his children that He will dwell in them: Satan seeks to dwell among sinners, especially sexual sinners. This is why whoremongers and adulterers are ever in the presence of the devil.

In fact, fornicators and adulterers have sacrificed themselves and their seed to the devil. Through prostitution, families, and nations, and even generations can be sold out to Satan *(Nahum 3:4)*.

Anyone caught in that web of Satan should await great tribulation from God *(Revelations 2:22)*, except they repent of their deeds.

SEX: A GIFT OF LIFE FROM GOD

The greatest and ultimate expression of love toward each other between husband and wife, as given to mankind by God, is sex. It is the cleaving together in body and in spirit. It puts a seal of love between husband and wife.

> *Lust leads to hatred. It is influenced by Satan. It is sinful; and it leads to death.*

"Husbands must love their wives and wives must reverence their husbands. The Bible says whoever loves his wife loves himself. For no man ever yet hated his own flesh; but nourishes and cherishes it even as the Lord, the church; for we are members of his body, of his flesh and of his bones. For this cause shall a man leave his father and mother and shall be joined to his wife and they two shall be one flesh. This is a great mystery concerning Christ and his Church" (Ephesians 5:26-32).

This scripture expresses the mystery of love between Christ and the church. And the true love between husband and wife is a replica of that wonderful mystery. True love is demonstrated by husbands and wives through sex. When love is genuine, it grows and grows and grows, even to everlasting. It does not fade away,

The Mystery of Sex

nor does it depreciate; it elongates into eternity. The pleasure cannot be expressed in tangible terms. It cannot be explained. It is like heaven on earth. It can be wonderful, glorious, and lovely.

When a couple are genuinely in love with each other, nothing can separate them. The devil cannot even come between them, if they are grounded in the word and the truth of God.

This kind of love can only come from God. The Bible says, *"He that loves not knows not God, for God is Love" (1 John 4:8)*. True and genuine love can only come from God. There is no fear in love, but perfect love casts out fear.

Whosoever dwells in love dwells in God and God in him. When a man loves his wife, he will not do her any evil. He will not go after another woman outside his home. The wife will not do any evil against her husband. She will reverence her husband, care for him, and entreat him with all love and humility in every circumstance. The two will not deny each other nor allow each other to be tempted by Satan.

> *Lust ends in hatred whereas true love releases greater love and it gets stronger.*

"The wife has not power of her own body, but the husband and likewise also the husband has not power of his own body but the wife. Defraud you not one the other, except it be with consent for a time, that you may give yourselves to fasting and prayer, and come together again, that Satan tempt you not for your incontinency" (1 Corinthians 7:4-5).

The above scripture is saying that the two are in one flesh and that they are part of each other. No one has power over his or her body again. The husband's body has been given to the wife, while that of the wife has been pledged to the husband. No one has a right to say "no" to the other when each knocks, except by mutual agreement. The union would wax stronger and stronger as the couple grow in grace in the Lord, strongly united.

> Another reference to sexual intercourse in marriage is "go in to her".

THE EVIL EFFECT OF LUST THAT ENDS IN MARRIAGE

What is lust? Let us consider some scriptures, to have a proper understanding of what lust is.

"But everyman is tempted, when he is drawn away of his own LUST and enticed. Then when LUST has conceived, it brings forth sin, and sin when it is finished brings forth death" (James 1:1-15).

Lust, according to this scripture, is the fulfillment of sinful desires. It is usually accompanied with sin. It is always contrary to the precepts given by God. It is always against the law of God and His commandment. Lust is the fulfillment of the canal desires. It is the work of the flesh, which is always against the spirit. It brings out sins hidden in the flesh.

The fallen nature of man is manifested through lust to sin, and sin leads to death. Many people commit adultery and fornication through the power of flesh and the lust thereof.

The Mystery of Sex

Let us consider some characters in the Bible who lusted after members of the opposite sex.

Joseph was sold into slavery in Egypt. He found himself in the home of Potiphar, an officer of Pharaoh. He was made an overseer in that home, and over everything his master had. And the Lord blessed the Egyptian's home for Joseph's sake, for Joseph was a godly person and well favored.

In *Genesis 39:7*, the Bible says,

"And it came to pass after these things that his master's wife cast her eyes upon Joseph; and she said, lie with me."

> Sexual intercourse between man and woman could mean raising up an altar to the Lord or to the devil.

This woman cast her eyes upon the young man, Joseph, not minding his status. She lusted after Joseph and wanted to lure him into sin against God and against her husband. Many women still do this. They would invite their husband's driver into their bedroom to commit adultery with him. Thank God, Joseph refused and did not hearken to her to lie by her or to be with her. He obeyed the commandment of God that says, "Flee fornication," and he fled.

Also a man in the Bible lusted after his stepsister whom he raped, thereby committing fornication with her. The man, Amnon, paid dearly with his life. Absalom, a son of David, had a fair sister, whose name was Tamar. And Amnon, also a son of David, loved her.

Amnon so much fell sick for his sister, Tamar, who was a virgin, that he desired to have sex with her at any cost. Then his satanic and subtle friend, Jonadab, wrongly advised him on how to fulfill his lustful desire.

> *But to "lie with," or "lay with her" is in the context of sexual immorality which leads to judgements from God that results in destruction.*

And Jonadab advised him, "Lay down in your bed and pretend you are sick, and when your father comes to see you, say to him, 'I pray you let my sister, Tamar come and give me meat, and dress the meal in my sight that I may see it and eat it at her hand.'" In verse 10, "Amnon said to Tamar, 'bring the meat into the chamber that I may eat of your hand.' And Tamar took the cakes which she had made and brought them into the chamber to Amnon her brother. And when she had brought them to him to eat, he took hold of her and said to her, 'Come lie with me, my sister.' Tamar refused and advised him to speak to the king his father, for he would not withhold her from him.

"Amnon did not hearken to her voice; however, being stronger than her, he forced her, and lay with her" (2 Samuel 13:1-14).

As soon as he successfully had his way, hatred set in. Then Amnon hated her exceedingly. The hatred he had for her was even greater than the love he previously confessed to her.

The Mystery of Sex

Lust leads to hatred. It is influenced by Satan. It is sinful, and it leads to death.

Lust is not love. Sisters should be able to differentiate between love and lust and not allow themselves to be used by any man to satisfy his sexual urge.

A lot of people have entered into marital covenant, led by lust rather than love. Today, their marriage is like hell on earth. The lust that brought them into wedlock has left them in regret and with bitter hatred for each other. God certainly cannot be in any marriage resulting from lust. It is the devil that presides over such marriages.

> *Sex has the capability to keep the home peaceful.*

Many husbands and wives compound their marital problem by going outside the marriage to look for satisfaction, thereby multiplying iniquities. This kind of practice provokes the anger of God against those who engage in it. Unless those in the practice repent and pray to God to heal their home, they will suffer under the wrath of God. Until God in His mercy comes to their rescue, peace will be far from their home.

Bachelors and spinsters must not allow their lustful desires to becloud their godly sense of reasoning. Amnon paid dearly, for Absalom, the elder brother of Tamar, killed him for defiling his sister, Tamar *(2 Samuel 13:28)*. Lust brings instant hatred whereas true love releases greater love, and it becomes stronger.

A brother and sister affianced to each other should be very weary of the lust of the flesh or lustful desires lest they should fall into sexual sin and hate each other. Hatred resulting from lust can bring an end to their courtship, or even marriage.

SEXUAL INTERCOURSE AS AN ACT OF BLOOD COVENANT

> *... of a truth there is no hiding place for sexual sinners.*

As soon as a woman is rightly joined to a man in marriage, the two enter into blood covenant because they are no longer two but one flesh.

For this cause shall a man leave his father and mother and shall be joined to his wife and they shall be one flesh.

Sexual intercourse is a means of entering into a blood covenant.

Once they have been joined together and have actually entered into that blood covenant, neither of the two has power over his/her own body.

"Let the husband render to the wife due benevolence and likewise also the wife, to her husband" (1 Corinthians 7:3).

This scripture says that in marriage, sex is a fundamental right under the covenant. The husband has every right to demand for sex from the woman, and the woman has no right to say no. Likewise, the woman has every right to demand for sex from the man, and the man has no right to say no. Sexual intercourse therefore is the fundamental right of each.

The Mystery of Sex

All women who use sex to control their husbands, or sometimes deny their husbands, are committing a serious sin against God, their own body, and against their marriage.

The so-called busy executives who leave their wives in the cold for meetings or functions do breach their marital covenants. This thing should not be so.

"Defraud you not one the other, except it be for with consent for a time that you may give yourselves to fasting and prayer; and come together again that Satan tempt you not for your incontinency" (1 Corinthians 7:5).

All the ministers of God, pastors, and evangelists who get so busy to the extent of denying their spouses of their rights in marriage must make amends at the home front. This denial can lead to confusion, which will threaten the peace of God in the home.

> *All the men and women who have secret extramarital affairs are just deceiving themselves. To be very honest; nothing is secret, after all.*

Often women cause trouble in the home, especially when they are denied sex. But they do not admit that the cause of their action is sexual denial. Sex has the capability to keep the home peaceful. And it is important because the home must be at peace before there can be peace in the larger society, the church, the office, et cetera.

It is important to know certain deep things about how the life of man affects the entire creation, both here on Earth and in heaven above.

"For there are three that bear record in heaven; the father, the Word and the Holy Ghost, and these three are one. And there are three that bear witness in earth; the spirit and the water and the blood, and these three agree in one" (1 John 5:7-8).

> *Anything you do with your body in sin will put your generation into serious spiritual problems with God.*

If one considers this scripture in the context of sexual activity, whether marital, pre-marital, or extramarital, one will discover that every action of man is transmitted both to the heaven above and to the earth. When I say the earth, I mean on and under the earth.

When someone is having sex secretly with somebody, the action is being transmitted to the Creator, even to the entire creation. Of a truth, there is no hiding place for sexual sinners.

To interpret the scripture above in the context of sexual intercourse: The Father bears record, the Word bears record, and the Holy Ghost bears record. The three agree as one. The Father is in the heaven, and His word covers both the heaven and the earth.

Even the words you speak to the man or the woman are related to the Word you refuse to obey. The words are then reported in heaven, testifying against you.

The Mystery of Sex

The Holy Ghost that moves across the whole earth, which may have spoken to your conscience to no avail, will also report your action in Heaven.

During coitus, the spirit inside you, the water inside your body, and the blood in your flesh and bones, from which semen is produced, will also present a record of your action to the Father in heaven, to the Word, and to the Holy Ghost. If the witnesses of man are believed here on earth, how much greater is the witness of God.

David committed adultery with the wife of Uriah, the Hittite whom he murdered. And God said to him, *"For you did it secretly but I will do this thing before all Israel and before the sun"* (2 Samuel 12:12).

All men and women who have secret extramarital affairs are deceiving themselves. To be very honest, nothing is secret, after all.

> *True and genuine love can only come from God. There is no fear in love, but perfect love casts out fear.*

"There is nothing covered that shall not be revealed and hid that shall not be known" (Matthew 10:26).

If you go in to a prostitute or you leave your husband and elope with a strange man, even your own body will report you.

Consider this scripture: *"For the creature was made subject to vanity, not willingly"* (Romans 8:20).

Your breast that you give out to a man other than your husband is not happy about your action. God created it for your children and for your husband.

Therefore, if another man touches it, you subject it to bondage of corruption. And it will surely testify against you before God.

Your manhood, the symbol of your strength, the vehicle through which your generation shall come forth to fulfill the agenda of God Almighty here on earth, cannot be happy with you if you use it immorally. This has a very serious negative spiritual implication.

> *It is very important for us to appreciate the atoning works of Christ on the cross of Calvary.*

God told Abraham, *"And in your seed shall the nations of the earth be blessed, because you have obeyed my voice" (Genesis 22:18).*

If Abraham had given his manhood to a harlot and had discharged his seed into her, this promise of God for him would not have been fulfilled. Anything sinful you do with your body will put your generation into serious spiritual problems with God. This is because as you are guilty and punishable, so is your generation.

Consider this scripture:

"And as I may say, Levi also who receives tithes, paid tithes in Abraham. 'For he was yet in the loins of his father, when Melchisedek met him'" (Hebrews 7:9-10).

This scripture is saying that Levi, who was the son of Jacob, the son of Isaac, the son of Abraham, paid tithes to Melchisedek, through Abraham his great grandfather. Abraham had not even given birth to Isaac, Levi's grandfather, when he met Melchisedek, the Priest of the Most High God who prayed for him:

The Mystery of Sex

"Blessed is Abram of the Most High God, Possessor of heaven and Earth" (Genesis 14:19).

It was this Priest of the Most High God that came back to the world through the lineage of Abraham as the Savior of the whole world, our High Priest, the Lord Jesus Christ.

If Abraham had ever lived a filthy life, the most Holy, the King of kings and the Lord of lords, would not have had anything to do with him. God probably would have visited his children with the iniquity of their father, even to the fourth generation.

Your seed is your might and the beginning of your strength. It is the excellency of your dignity and power. Therefore, do not pour it out immorally. The Bible says, *"Give not your strength to women nor your ways to that which destroys kings" (Proverbs 31:3).*

When you subject any part of you to corruption, through sexual immorality, do you think you can be guiltless? That part of you that are meant for a specific assignment from the Lord will surely cry against you.

The Bible says, "For we know that the whole creation groans and travails in pain together until now" (Romans 8:22).

Your manhood, the symbol of your strength, which you use as an instrument of sin and unrighteousness groans and travails in pain, and will surely cry against you.

Your hands, which you use immorally as an instrument of unrighteousness, should be kept holy and be used in adoration and praise of your Creator. So for using them in immoralities, to caress the body of agents of darkness, they will report and cry against you before the Almighty God. Satan, our enemy, knows this too well, having previously been with God. That is why he is happy that he has succeeded in leading man too far away from God through sin.

It is very important for us to appreciate the atoning work of Christ on the cross of Calvary, which gives us the opportunity to reconcile with God through the blood of the covenant that is shed for the remission of our sin. The blood is made available to mankind to make us whole again before the Holy God, standing blameless and acquitted.

Prayers

Scriptures: Psalm 51—Repentance

Create in me a clean heart Oh Lord
And renew a right spirit within me
Cast me not away from your presence
Oh Lord
Take not your Holy Spirit from me
Restore to me, your joy of
your Salvation
And renew a right spirit within me

Prayer Points

1. Oh Lord, forgive me all my sexual sins, in the name of Jesus.
2. Oh Lord! By your mercy, redeem me from the grip of Satan.
3. Oh Lord, By your outstretched arm deliver me from the bondage of sexual perversion and prison, in the name of Jesus.

The Mystery of Sex

4. By the blood of Jesus, cleanse me from blood guiltiness, in the name of Jesus.
5. Let the redemptive power in the blood of Jesus visit me and my generation, in the name of Jesus.
6. Thank God for His power to deliver from bondage.
7. I break myself from every spirit of sexual perversion, in the name of Jesus.
8. I release myself from spiritual pollution emanating from my past sins of fornication and sexual immorality, in the name of Jesus.
9. I release myself from every ancestral pollution, in the name of Jesus.
10. I release myself from every dream pollution in the name of Jesus.
11. I command every evil plantation of sexual perversion in my life to come out with all its root, in the name of Jesus.
12. Every spirit of sexual perversion, working against my life, be paralyzed and get out of my life, in the name of Jesus.
13. Every demon of sexual perversion assigned to my life, be bound in the name of Jesus.
14. Father Lord, let the power of sexual perversion oppressing my life receive the fire of God and be roasted, in the name of Jesus.
15. Every inherited demon of sexual perversion in my life, receive the arrows of fire and remain permanently bound in the name of Jesus.
16. I command every force or power of sexual perversion to come against themselves, in the name of Jesus.
17. Father Lord, let every demonic stronghold built in my life by the spirit of sexual perversion be pulled down, in the name of Jesus.

18. Let every power of sexual perversion that has summoned my life be shattered to pieces, in the name of Jesus.
19. Let my soul be delivered from the force of sexual perversion, in the name of Jesus.
20. Let the Lord God of Elijah arise with a strong hand against every spirit wife/husband and power of sexual perversion, in the name of Jesus.
21. I break the hold of any evil power over my life, in the name of Jesus.
22. I nullify every effect of the bite of sexual perversion upon my life, in the name of Jesus.
23. Every evil stranger, satanic deposit in my life, I command you to be paralyzed and get out of my life, in the name of Jesus.
24. Holy Ghost Fire, purge my life completely, in the name of Jesus.
25. I claim my complete deliverance, in the name of Jesus, from the spirit of fornication and sexual immorality. in the name of Jesus.
26. Let my eyes be delivered from lustfulness, in the name of Jesus.
27. As from today, let my eyes be controlled by the Holy Spirit, in the name of Jesus.
28. Holy Ghost Fire, fall upon my eyes and burn to ashes every evil force and satanic power, in the name of Jesus.
29. I move from bondage to liberty in every area of my life, in the name of Jesus.
30. Thank God for answers to prayers.

CHAPTER FOUR

Sexual Intercourse in Marriage

The Mystery of Marriage

A lot of people go into marriage without understanding its purpose and what it should be. Quite a lot of people enter into it only to find out later in life that they have made the greatest mistake of their lives.

In fact, the devil has a proper understanding of what marriage should be. He knows that many people who go into marriage do so in great ignorance. He, therefore, uses the state of spiritual ignorance adequately to destabilize many marriages, to fulfill his plans against the children of God as contained in *Psalm 2:3*, *"Let us break their bands asunder and cast away their cords from us."*

Many marriages have been broken asunder by the enemy to facilitate the job of the enemy, which is to lead men to eternal destruction.

It is therefore important that all should have the idea of God's purpose for marriage and what marriage stands for, especially those who want to serve God and hope to reign with Him in His everlasting Kingdom.

Marriage is the first institution ordained by God Almighty. The institution came into existence before the church. It is the union of man and woman, into one flesh, fussed together in body, soul, and spirit.

God created man in His own image. He formed man out of the dust of the ground and breathed into his nostrils. Man then became a living soul.

> *It is the will of God for man to have a job to do and a home to keep before thinking of marriage.*

"And the Lord God took the man and put him into the garden of Eden to dress it and to keep it" (Genesis 2:15).

Our God is a God of preparation. Before God created man and his wife, He had prepared a very beautiful place for them to live and to enjoy their lives therein. God placed man inside a beautiful garden "to dress it and to keep it." In order words, God gave man a job to do and a home to keep. It is the will of God for man to have a job to do and a home to keep before thinking of marriage.

God gave man a standing commandment and rule to follow to live a successful life in the garden, the house given to him. This means God is part of the family. God is to guide man on how to operate in the

The Mystery of Sex

home given to him. God even sometimes came down at the cool of the day to have fellowship with man, whom He created for the purpose of declaring His Glory.

When everything was created, God observed, *"It is not good that man should be alone, I will make help meet for him" (Genesis 2:18).*

God took a decision to create a helper suitable for man for the purpose of fellowship and to fulfill the commandment of God and his blessings upon man and all things which he had created, which was spoken thus:

"Be fruitful and multiply and replenish the earth" (Genesis 1:28).

God created a helper suitable for Adam for companionship, fruitfulness, multiplication, and replenishment.

> *God created a helper suitable for Adam for fellowship fruitfulness, multiplication and replenishment.*

"And the Lord God caused a deep sleep to fall upon Adam and he slept and took one of his ribs and closed up the flesh thereof; And the ribs which the Lord had taken from man, made he a woman and brought her to the man.

"And Adam said; This is now bone of my bones, and flesh of my flesh; she shall be called woman, because she was taken out of man.

"Therefore shall a man leave his father and his mother and shall cleave to his wife, and they shall be one flesh.

And they were both naked, the man and his wife, and were not ashamed" (Genesis 2:22-25).

Marriage is an institution created by God so that those in it may have fellowship with Him and so that they will worship Him and remain in His presence. Marriage therefore brings about a family unit, which on its own is a small church unit.

In marriage, the husband and wife have certain responsibilities. God ordained such responsibilities, and no one can change them. If someone acts contrary to God's ordinance, he brings confusions into his/her home. And the devil will take over.

> *To follow the counsel of God in marriage is to prosper in it. And to prosper in marriage is to prosper in life and, ultimately, in eternity.*

When the devil, the adversary, takes over, he will lead the couple by the nose to a place of destruction. This is why the devil attacks marriages fiercely, using every trick and weapon available. The devil knows that once a marriage is attacked, every other target of attack in the lives of the couple will just be a walk over.

The devil is an unfair fighter. He uses the ignorance of human beings to attack them. In fact, the ignorance of man is his mountain.

To follow the counsel of God in marriage is to prosper in it. And to prosper in marriage is to prosper in life and, ultimately, in eternity.

"Counsel in the heart of man is like deep water; but a man of understanding will draw it out" (Proverbs 20:5)

The Mystery of Sex

When a man or woman of understanding gets into God's counsel, he or she will not despise it, for the counsel of God will surely stand.

Marriage is an institution ordained by God Almighty. The ordinance of God for it must be the rock on which all may stand. The word of God is the secret of success and the sacred constitution for living. As a matter of necessity, any wise man or woman who wants to go into marriage must understand the doctrine of God for marriage. He or she must understand the plan of the devil against marriage. He must also understand the operations of the devil and guide, diligently, against the enemy's operations.

There are some anti-success forces that work against marriages. These are human agents or personalities that work for anti-marriage forces. As far as these agents are concerned, they don't have any plan for peaceful marriage, nor are they ready to obey God. The only plan they have is to steal other people's marriage or to be yoked to their victims in marriage in order to torment them with affliction, frustration, and poverty. These agents of darkness target the children of Most High God, especially those chosen by God for specific assignments. The target children are often the chosen prophets and prophetesses of God.

> *There are human agents of darkness all over the place.*

The marriage of these people is the target of the devil and his agents. This is to hinder the assignment God has committed into their hands.

It is very sad that men and women whom God chooses to serve Him rarely easily discern the call of God and His purpose for their lives. But the agents of darkness can identify them and God's purpose for their lives. They therefore pursue these children of God with all might that they may get married to them and abort their destinies.

The main target in the lives of these children of God is their marriage. Once the devil succeeds in manipulating them into marrying agents of darkness, it becomes hard for them to fulfill God's purpose for their lives. This is why it is essential to receive one's calling before marriage so that one can rightly pray for the partner who will assist one in the ministry, and one will not end up with a partner that will deliberately destroy one's ministry

> *Marriage must be covenanted prayerfully, discreetly, soberly and diligently, with God's guidance.*

There are agents of darkness all over the place. In their thoughts, actions, and entire living, they stand against God and His purpose. God is never in their thoughts, and they are never ready to obey Him.

This is why a sister who loves God with all her might can be manipulated into marrying an occult man who will promptly order her to stop calling the name of Jesus in his house and prevent her from going to church. Such sisters would now find themselves in a serious marital bondage.

The Mystery of Sex

The outstretched arm of God will deliver as many sisters as are reading this book in such a situation, in Jesus name (Amen). However, if such sisters don't learn how to pray but remain ignorant of what to do, they will not only fail in their life endeavors, they will also fail God and end up in hell fire. This is because the devil has succeeded in yoking them in marriage to his agents.

A sister was offered a sum of two billion, five hundred million Naira by her husband to renounce her Christian faith and stop calling the name of Jesus in his house. The sister was astonished and confused. She ran to her pastor who told her that her husband wanted to purchase her salvation and heavenly joy with 2.5 billion Naira.

The sister, having been advised by her pastor not to sell her salvation and her God, had to run out of her matrimonial home.

> *I advise all bachelors and spinsters who read this book to pray very well before entering into marital bondage.*

Many great men of God have been yoked in marriage to Jezebel. This is more serious, because the Jezebel will not open up. Rather, she will always secretly frustrate the life and the ministry of the man of God. This is why marriage must not be entered into through the will of the flesh.

Marriage must be covenanted prayerfully, discreetly, soberly, and diligently with God's guidance. It must not be entered into without adequate understanding of what it is. Once it has been covenanted, there is no going back. And it takes the grace of God for one to be delivered from evil marital bondage

The sister whose husband wanted to purchase her salvation suffered so many things. It was after hot prayers that the man came up with the idea of luring her away from Jesus with money. It was the counsel of the Holy Spirit that she should depart since the man was not ready for God.

> *All witches and wizards and those who have familiar spirits are abominable before God.*

There are many witches and wizards in the society, people who have sold off their souls to Satan. People who have vowed and covenanted their souls, body and spirit to Satan, and have decided never to turn against him but to serve him all the days of their lives in this world and in the world which is to come. Satan has promised them a kingdom of their own in the world to come. These people can never repent. Sometimes they marry inside the church. In fact, they are workers in the church. They can seem to be very zealous for God and His work, but their ultimate goal is to pollute the church of God.

If a prayer less child of God gets yoked to such people in marriage, such a child of God will experience hell on earth. All the laws and divine marital precepts will turn against such a person. It then becomes easy for satanic agents to execute their plans. It is only God Almighty that can deliver him/her.

The Mystery of Sex

However, God will not forsake His people. He will surely deliver His own, but the flesh will suffer. But if the children of God in marital bondage do not pray enough or cannot hear God clearly, they may end up losing their lives, ministries, and even their positions in heaven. The enemy has entered into their innermost beings, like rottenness inside the bone. It is only God who can deliver them.

I advise all bachelors and spinsters who have read this book to pray very well before entering into marital bondage. Check out what the Lord God says in this scripture:.

"You shall say to the children of Israel, whosoever he be of the children of Israel or of the strangers that Sojourn in Israel that gives any of his seed to Molech, he shall surely be put to death, the people of that land shall stone him with stones.

> *If God is interested in fragments of bread, how much more will he be interested in human seeds created in His image. Somebody wasted the seed of his body (his sperm) deliberately by spilling it on the ground and God killed him.*

"And I will set my face against that man, and I will cut him off from away his people, because he had given of his seed to Molech, to defile My sanctuary, and to profane My holy name.

"And I will set My face against that man and against his family and will cut him off, and all that go awhoring

after him to commit whoredom with Molech, from among their people.

"And the soul that turns after such as have familiar spirits and after wizards to go awhoring after them. I will even set my face against that soul and will cut him off from among his people" (Leviticus 20:2-6).

Molech is the idol of the Ammonites, a strange god. Our God is a jealous God, who would not allow any of His children to follow after strange gods. All the gods of the nations are idols and the works of men. Allowing one's seed to pass through the Molech is a serious matter with the Lord.

> *For anyone to partake in that glorious marriage, the status of his robe before God is a determining factor. It must be white, glorious and without blemish.*

When a child of God is joined to a strange personality, in spirit, soul, and body through sexual sin, he invites grave punishments from the Almighty. All witches and wizards and those who have familiar spirits are abominable before God. They serve another god, which is Satan. So sleeping with such personalities is tantamount to joining them or allowing one's seed to pass through the fire to Molech, which is against the commandment of God Almighty *(Leviticus 20:2).*

Every seed of your body is very important to the Lord. You must therefore not allow any seed of your body to be poured out into immorality: adultery or fornication. It provokes the anger of the Lord.

The Mystery of Sex

"A seed shall serve Him; it shall be accounted to the Lord for a generation" (Psalm 22:30).

A single seed in your body is a generation, as far as Heaven is concerned. When Jesus fed about five thousand men, excluding women and children, with five barley loaves of bread and two fishes, they were all filled. Then Jesus said to his disciples, *"Gather up the fragments that remain that nothing be lost" (John 6:9-12).* If God is interested in fragments of bread, how much more will he be interested in human seeds created in His image.

Somebody wasted the seed of his body (his sperm) deliberately by spilling it on the ground. And God killed him.

"Judah said to Onan, 'Go in to your brother's wife and marry her and raise up seed to your brother. The brother of Onan, Er, had just died because of his wickedness before the Lord.'

> *A holy marriage here between husband and wife is the shadow of the great marriage between Christ and His church.*

"And Onan knew that the seed should not be his and it came to pass when he went in to his brother's wife [while having sex with the brother's wife] that he spilled it on the ground lest he should give seed to his brother [He poured out the sperm on the floor].

"And the thing which he did displeased the Lord, wherefore He slew him also [God killed him] (Genesis 38:7-10).

If anyone, either man or woman, allows that seed be poured out into immorality, such a person provokes the anger of God.

Marriage is a mystery. It signifies the union of man with the Lord God. It is also complementary to the union of Christ with the church. Therefore, anyone who brings defilement into the union shall be cut off from among his people.

Christ represents the Father of Glory, and that same Christ is seen as the bridegroom of God's people. The church is the bride of Christ. The Bride of Christ must be thoroughly purged, holy and free from any abominable things. The bride must be sanctified, thoroughly cleansed, that Jesus might present it to Himself a glorious church. The church should not have any spot, wrinkle, or any such thing, but should be holy and without blemish.

To partake in this glorious vision, no one should allow himself to be defiled. Once someone is defiled, he or she shall be cut off.

> *Anyone who wants to be united with the Lord should ensure an honourable marriage, and that the bed remains undefiled.*

Defilement, however, can happen through marriage or sexual immoralities. Therefore, all prospective spouses must know the spiritual status of their partners before they are joined together.

MARRIAGE AS A UNION WITH GOD

Marriage is the institution that brings the church

and God Almighty together, through the slain Lamb whose blood washed off the filthiness of man before God. God, being a Holy God, is in marriage with the virgin Church; glorious, spotless, and without wrinkles or blemish, but holy.

Marriage is also that institution that brings about the union of God and His people. It is the shadow of things to come in the hereafter, which is the marriage of the Lamb. For anyone to partake in that glorious marriage, the status of his robe before God is a determining factor. It must be white, glorious, and without blemish.

> **Defilement of any sort will be cut off from among the people of God.**

"After this I behold and lo a great multitude, which no man could number of all nations and kindred and people and tongues, stood before the lambs clothed with white robes and palms in their hands.

"And cried with a loud voice saying: Salvation to our God which sits upon the throne and to the Lamb. And all the Angels stood round about the throne, and about the elders and the four beasts and fell before the throne on their faces and worshipped God saying: Amen. Blessing and glory and wisdom, and thanksgiving and honour and power and might be to our God for ever and ever.

"And one of the Elders answered saying to me what are these which are arrayed in white robes and whence came they? And I said to him: sir, you know. And he said to me. These are they which came out of great tribulation and have washed their robes and made them white in the blood of the Lamb.

"Therefore are they before the throne of God, and serve him day and night in his temple and he that sits on the throne shall dwell among them.

"They shall hunger no more neither thirsty any more, neither shall the sun light on them nor any heat.

"For the lamb which is in the midst of the throne shall feed them and shall lead them to living fountain of waters and God shall wipe away all tears from their eyes" (Revelations 7:9-17).

> God has made every man his representative in every home, though He watches all.

A holy marriage between husband and wife is the shadow of the great marriage between Christ and His church.

This is why the Bible says, "Wives, submit yourselves to your own husband, as to the Lord. For the husband is the head of the wife, even as Christ is the head of the church, and he is the savior of the body. Therefore as the church is subject to Christ, so let wives be to their own husbands in everything.

"Husbands, love your wives even as Christ also loved the church and gave himself for it. That He might sanctify and cleanse it with the washing of water by the word. That He might present it to himself a glorious church, not having spot or wrinkle or any such thing but that it should be holy and without blemish.

"So ought men love their wives as their own bodies. He that loves his wife loves himself. For no man ever yet hated

The Mystery of Sex

his own flesh, but nourishes and cherishes it, even as the Lord the Church. For we are members of His body, of His flesh and of His bones. For this cause shall a man leave his father and mother, and shall be joined to his wife, and they two shall be one flesh. This is a great mystery: but I speak concerning Christ and the church" (Ephesians 5:22-32).

This scripture brings out the fundamental reason why a man should leave his father and mother and be joined to his wife, to ultimately be united with the Lord, being a member of the body of Christ, which is the church. This explains why the devil attacks Christian marriages. The devil knows that the success of Christian marriages is fundamental to success of Christians in the kingdom of God in heaven.

> *The fire of jealousy which is described as having a most vehement flame is such that cannot be quenched. It is stubborn, strong and cruel.*

Anyone who wants to be united with the Lord should ensure both an honorable marriage and that the bed remains undefiled. Defilement of any sort will lead to being cut off from among the people of God.

The greatest strategy of the devil to make men and women defile their robes is through illicit sexual intercourse.

Hear this: Husband and wife who are legally married could still, through the doctrine of the devil, involve themselves in illicit sexual intercourse that brings defilement. These are oral sex, masturbation, anal sex, lesbianism, watching of pornographic film or video together, sleeping together during the wife's period of menstruation. These bring defilement, and they that do such shall be cut off from among the people of God called the church.

The question to you, as you are reading this book is: do you commit these sins with your wife or your husband? Repent fast. The scripture says:

> *Anywhere the sin of adultery or sexual sin persists, it brings sword upon the home, the family and the nation.*

"I beseech you therefore, brethren by the mercies of God, that you present your bodies a living sacrifice, Holy, acceptable to God which is your reasonable service. And be not conformed to this world; but be you transformed by the renewing of your mind; that you may prove what is good and acceptable and perfect will of God" (Romans 12:1-2).

Any form of sexual perversion between a legally married husband and wife can never qualify them to enter into the acceptable and perfect will of God. Let this be clear in your spirit as you read on.

Sisters who refuse to obey their husbands at home are only preparing themselves to be united with the devil, not God. If care is not taken by the man, if he allows himself to be ruled by the woman, he could be dragged to hell by her.

God told Adam, "Because you have hearkened to the voice of your wife." Then curses followed (Genesis 3:17).

If a woman refuses to submit to her husband and she's indulging in sinful acts and her husband fails to avert the situation, God will make the man, not the woman, answerable for such acts. God has made every man His representative in every home, though he watches all.

If the situation prevalent in a home is contrary to God's will, God will quietly depart from that home, and the devil will totally step in. We all know the situation where devil rules.

> *Whosoever despises the law of God is inviting the sword upon his house, his family and his nation, and even his generations.*

THE FAMILY UNIT, THE CHURCH, AND THE WORLD AT LARGE

The family unit is the fragment that constitutes the church, and even the larger society that makes up the entire world. The devil knows that the peace in each family will eventually result in peace in the church and the world at large. His fight against the world's peace and therefore starts with the family unit. The devil ensures that he influences each family against the commandments of God so as to erode the peace of God in them and the entire world at large.

The strategy of the devil is to push man into sin against God and fellow man, so as to bring evil upon them. The most effective weapon of fulfillment of his wicked desire for man is illicit sexual intercourse vis-à-vis adultery with neighbors' wives or husbands. The devil knows the power and the rage of jealousy.

The Bible says, *"Jealousy is cruel as the grave, the coals thereof are coals of fire which has a most vehement flame" (Song of Solomon 8:6).*

> *Children born into the polygamous family live in violence, discord, fear, disaffection, envy and all sorts of evil.*

Check out the words used to describe jealousy in the scripture above. They are very serious words. The fire of jealousy, which is described as having a most vehement flame, is such that it cannot be quenched. It is stubborn, strong, and cruel. Jealousy is also described as "the rage of a man," which makes him willing to revenge *(Proverbs 6:34).*

The power of jealousy has the ability to devour, to consume, and to destroy utterly. The Bible refers to the spirit of jealousy in Numbers 5:14. When the spirit of jealousy comes upon a man for his wife, having found out that she has been defiled, the curse that follows has the ability to pursue, overtake, and destroy. It has the ability to cause the thigh of the woman in question to rot and her belly to swell *(Numbers 5:21).*

Once this spirit of jealousy is invoked, it can bring disaster upon the entire family, even upon generations.

David was influenced by Satan as he walked upon the roof of his house one evening and beheld a beautiful

The Mystery of Sex

woman, bathing naked. And David failed to terminate the agenda of the devil for his life and his household. Rather, he sent and inquired about the woman and was told she was the wife of Uriah, the Hittite. Still, David did not stop, knowing that she was a married woman, but he sent a messenger to call her. And he committed adultery with her *(2 Samuel 11:4)*.

David, having known the woman, slept with her and impregnated her, while her husband was at the war front. In order to cover the sin, however, he recalled the husband of the woman from the war front and encouraged him to go in to his wife. But the faithful servant of the king would not go home to his wife while Israel, with the ark of the Lord, was in the open at the battlefield.

> *Sleeping with neighbours' wives is described as going upon hot coals of fire.*

"And Uriah said to David, 'The ark and Israel and Judah abide in tents; and my Lord Joab and the servants of my Lord, are encamped in the open fields, shall I go into my house, to eat, and to lie with my wife? As you live and your soul lives, I will not do this thing'" (2 Sam. 11:11).

And David plotted the death of his faithful servant, even after committing adultery with his wife, and the Lord's anger was kindled against David.

And the Lord spoke through his prophet Nathan to David saying:

"Why have you despised the commandment of the Lord, to do evil in his sight. You have killed Uriah the Hittite

with the sword and has taken his wife to be your wife and has slain him with the sword of the children of Ammon.

"Now therefore the sword shall never depart from your house because you have despised me."

The Lord went further and said *"Behold I will raise up evil against you in your own house, and I will take your wives before your eyes and give them to your neighbor, and he shall lie with your wives in the sight of the sun. For you did it secretly, but I will do this thing before Israel and before the sun"* (2 Samuel 9-12).

> Once a man is defiled, his entire home, both the wife and the children, shall be defiled, because a strange blood has been brought into the family, and defilement is now over the entire household.

This curse the Lord pronounced upon the house of David is still working even till date. The absence of peace in Jerusalem, the city of David, can be traced back to this curse upon the house of David.

The sin of adultery brings evil upon the family, even on the home of the culprit and his generations. It erodes the peace of God in the family unit and, by extension, erodes the peace in the church and the society at large.

Anywhere the sin of adultery or sexual sin persists, it brings sword upon the home, the family, and the nation. Check out the words of the curse pronounced again: "Now therefore the sword shall never depart from your house because you have despised me."

The Mystery of Sex

Whosoever despises the law of God is inviting the sword upon his house, his family, his nation, and even his generations.

When the peace of God departs from a family, the devil moves in and takes charge of that family. Sexual sin therefore brings multiple negative effects upon the entire family, the church, and the larger society.

The culture of polygamy starts with adultery with neighbor's wives. Some men covet their neighbors' wives, whom they later marry. Quite a lot of kings in Africa do this without inhibition or remorse. In fact, they arbitrarily exercise their authority and power over the weak. The Bible says they shall not be innocent.

> *A lot of men have killed their wives and children unknowingly through illicit sexual relationship, outside their marriage.*

"So he that goes into his neighbors' wife, whosoever touches her shall not be innocent" (Proverbs 6:29).

A lot of people are suffering today because of the misdeeds of their fathers and fore fathers. A lot of homes are filled with violence and evil that arose from sexual immoralities.

Many polygamous men have brought witches and satanic agents into their homes through sexual immorality. Everyone from a polygamous home has a serious battle to fight, as children born into the polygamous setting live in violence, discord, fear, disaffection, envy, and all sorts of evil.

The rage of jealousy as I said earlier is stubborn and devouring. It has the ability to disgrace and to inflict wounds. The spirit of jealousy can be invoked.

Something happened at Mushin (Lagos, Nigeria) sometime in 1985, which was widely reported in newspapers. A woman, a mother of four, and her man friend had sex in a battery charger's workshop. After the exercise, they discovered they could not detach from each other. And they were there naked. As they were struggling to break loose from each other, they fell upon a naked live wire and were electrocuted. It was a pathetic scene. People gathered to behold their naked remains, which were stuck together.

> *When a man sleeps with a prostitute, he defiles his own blood, and that of his wife and children.*

What happened to them? There is something called "Magun" in Yoruba land. It is a kind of spell that is cast upon a woman by a jealous husband suspicious of his wife. If that spell is upon a woman, and any man sleeps with her, he dies in the act.

The duo can stick together. Sometimes, the man can die instantly or gradually. At times, the man can start barking like a dog, or croaking like a fowl. The effect of the spell is dependent on its kind and the mandate assigned to it and the power behind it. It is this spell that caught up with the woman and the battery

The Mystery of Sex

charger, which made them stick together. It is only the man that cast the spell that can decree their freedom, according to the satanic mandate.

This spell has destroyed so many people especially in Africa. Many people who lived in adultery, meddling with their neighbors wives, have gone to the great beyond.

What is the power behind this spell? It is the spirit of jealousy that the Bible describes as cruel, grave, and having a vehement flame of fire.

> *The man could have ignorantly traded his entire family away for transient sexual pleasure.*

"For by means of a whorish woman, a man is brought to a piece of bread, and the adulteress will hunt for the precious life" (Proverbs 6:26).

Sleeping with neighbors' wives is described as going upon hot coals of fire

"Can a man take fire in his bosom and his clothes not be burned? Can one go upon hot coals, and his feet not be burned?" (Proverbs 27-28).

This spell that is sent to destroy has its foundation and mandate from the rage of jealousy.

"For jealousy is the rage of a man therefore he will not spare in the day of vengeance. He will not regard any ransom neither will he rest content, though you give many gifts" (Proverbs 6:34-35).

The way of transgressor is very hard. The man who obeys all the God's commandments can never find himself in any mess.

It is written: *"There shall no evil happen to the just but the wicked shall be filled with mischief"* *(Proverbs 12:21)*. It is wickedness that makes a man to lust after another man's wife.

> *... eyelids can be so powerful and full of the potential to lure men away from God.*

If any man says, "I don't go in to married women but unmarried girls or ladies," such a man cannot escape the consequences of sexual immorality.

A man who is married with children and goes out to strange women to defile himself would bring evil into his home through illicit sexual relations.

Once a man is defiled, his entire home, both the wife and the children, shall be defiled, because a strange blood has been brought into the family, and defilement is now over the entire household. A gate of violence and evil has been opened to the enemy, and the entire family is opened to attack.

This explains why formerly brilliant children suddenly become dull and start performing very poorly in the class. And the father might castigate them, not knowing that his relationship with a strange woman is the cause of their problem.

The children can lose their virtue once either of their parents is involved in extramarital sex. Some satanic agents have the power to inflict the wives and children of a man with whom they had extramarital affairs with strange sicknesses. As a result of this, many men have killed their wives and children unknowingly through sex outside marriage.

"Whosoever commits adultery with a woman lacks understanding: he that does it destroys his own soul" (Proverbs 6:32).

Adultery, which is extramarital sex, brings very grave consequences upon the man, the wife, the children, the entire family, and also the generations yet unborn.

> *Those ladies have succeeded in taking many men out of their matrimonial homes.*

THE SOUL TRADERS

The Bible talks about soul traders in *Revelations 18:11-13.*

"And the merchants of the earth shall weep and mourn over her; for no man buys their merchandise any more. The merchandise of gold, and silver, and precious stones and of pearls, and fine linen and purple, and silk, and scarlet, and all thine wood, and all manner vessels of ivory, and manner of vessels of most precious wood, and of brass, and iron, and marble. And cinnamon, and odours, and ointments, and frankincense, and wine, and oil; and fine flour, and wheat, and beast, and sheep, and horses, and chariots and slaves and SOULS OF MEN."

This scripture says there are merchants that merchandise in gold, silver, and souls of men. The question now is how do they trade—that is, buy and sell in souls of men?

The answer to this question can be found in *Nahum 3:1- 4*.

"Woe to the bloody city! it is all full of lies and robberies; the prey departs not; the noise of a whip, and the noise of the rattling of wheels and the prancing horses, and of the jumping chariots.

"The horseman lifts up both the bright sword and the glittering spear and there is a multitude of slain, and a great number of carcases; and there is none end of their corpses, they stumble upon their corpses."

> *If a man delights in sleeping with another man's wife, it is sure that his wife would be given to another man. It is a spiritual law.*

Why were these so? Why was there so much violence? Why did people die like flies? Why were so many roasted to death? Why were so many cries in different homes? Why were their corpses so much that they stumbled upon corpses and there was no end to these calamities? Why?

"It is because of the multitude of the whoredoms of the well favored harlots, the mistress of witchcraft that sells nations through her whoredoms, and families through her witchcrafts."

The souls of these men, women, and children had already been sold out through whoredom. Whoredom or prostitution defiles the blood, and the Bible says life is in the blood. Every form of sexual immorality therefore brings defilement to the blood and the life therein.

"And that same life is described as 'a vapour that appears for a little time, and then vanishes away'" (James 4:14).

When a man sleeps with a prostitute, he defiles his blood and that of his wife and children. The prostitute, being an agent of Satan, has the ability and the mandate to transfer every life in the man's family to the blood bank of Satan. The man gives the prostitute unhindered access to his blood and that of members of his family by having sex with her thereby pouring out his blood (sperm) into her. This is because the sperm (blood) will spiritually connect the man and his family members to the prostitute and her satanic mates in their coven.

> *If the cases of armed robbers molesting women in the presence of their husbands are traced very well, you'll discover that such occurs as a result of God's judgement against the husbands.*

Witchcraft and prostitution are two bedfellows. The man could have ignorantly traded his entire family away for transient sexual pleasure. Imagine such a foolish bargain!

There are many soul traders on our streets, moving from offices to offices, trading in the souls of men with Satan and getting riches, power, and influence, depending on how formidable they are in their business.

These girls are often very beautiful, tall, and fashionable, with unblemished skin. They are the dream of an average ignorant young man. Sometimes they come from the oceans, having no earthly parents, and they move about from offices to offices. By the time they are through with a man, his life will have been shredded out completely.

The Bible likens life to "a vapor that appears for a little time, and then vanishes away." Through the operation of prostitutes, a life can be caused to vanish away even before the Lord's appointed time. It is only those who are in the Lord and keep His commandments who are under His care and protection. An enemy of God is on his own and can be devoured by the roaring lion of the world at any time.

The so-called glamorous ladies who walk about the streets, to be very honest, are very deadly. The Bible says, "Lust not after her beauty in your heart, neither let her take you with her eyelids. *For by means of a whorish woman a man is brought to piece of bread, and the adulteress will hunt for the precious life"* (Proverbs 6:26).

This scripture is saying that eyelids can be so powerful and full of the potential to lure men away from their wives and God.

Many wives really have to pray for their husbands. A lot of homes have been broken. Those ladies have succeeded in taken away many men out of their matrimonial homes.

One of them confessed in a news magazine. She said she was like electricity and that she delighted in shocking and electrocuting housewives. As many housewives who had been electrocuted, the Lord shall restore them, in Jesus Name.

MARRIAGE MUST BE HONORABLE AND THE BED UNDEFILED

Hebrews 13:4 says, "Marriage is honorable in all and the bed undefiled but, whore mongers and adulterers God will judge."

Apart from the fact that illicit extramarital sex brings violence and opens the gate to Satan and his hosts, God also will join in the fight and battle against prostitutes and adulterers.

The Bible says, *"It's fearful thing, to fall into the hands of the living God" (Hebrews 10:31).* When God fights, who can deliver from His hands? No one. In fact, it will make things easy for Satan. This is why Satan uses sex as the most destructive weapon in these last days.

> *Adultery starts from the heart. Once a thought of adultery enter into one's heart, and it is meditated upon; as far as God is concerned, that heart is already defiled.*

Any man or woman found in adultery is provoking God to anger. Marriage is very sacred and must be honored by both parties. The bed must be kept holy and undefiled.

Some women, who are married to busy executives, are influenced by Satan to engage in extramarital sex.

Many of them engage in this illicit affair for nothing but sexual incontinence.

That a husband does not perform up to expectation does not give the wife the liberty of seeking sexual pleasure outside her home. Any woman who does this is making a coffin for her husband and children. The sorrow that will result is more profound than the pleasure she derives in the sexual vice.

> *Some people are fond of cursing others at the slightest offence, bringing defilement into their life and the lives of others.*

Marriage must be kept honorable. The bed must be kept holy, and couples must pray hard for themselves. If the behavior of your husband toward you is cold, go into prayer. And the Lord will touch him and heal your marriage.

God hates every act of adultery seriously. Therefore, extra-marital sexual practices attract severe punishment form God.

God said to Abimelech in a dream, when he took Sarah, Abraham's wife, *"Behold, you are but a dead man, for the woman, which you have taken; for she's a man's wife" (Genesis 20:3)*. Abimelech had not touched the woman, yet God had already started the process of fighting for Abraham. This means if anyone attempts to defile the wife of a man who is righteous before God and keeps His commandments, God will always fight on behalf of the man, even without his knowledge.

The problem is that many men whose wives are sometimes caught in adultery are unrighteous before

God. God therefore operates as a spectator in their case.

If a man delights in sleeping with another man's wife, other men will take his wife to bed. It is not a curse. It is a spiritual law.

God told David who committed adultery with Uriah's wife that *"I will take your wife before your eyes and give them to your neighbor and he shall lie with your wives in the sight of sun" (2 Samuel 12:11)*.

If you trace the cases of armed robbers molesting women in the presence of their husbands very well, you'll discover that such occurs as a result of God's judgment against the husbands, who must have committed adultery with other men's wives *(2 Samuel 12:11)*.

Sin is the cause of affliction. So everything that goes wrong in the physical can be traced to the spiritual realm.

> *Anything God calls an abomination must be avoided seriously by anyone who intends to dwell in God's presence.*

The Bible says, *"Fools, because of their transgression and because of their iniquities are afflicted" (Psalm 107:17)*.

MARRIAGE MUST BE HONORABLE AND BED UNDEFILED

WHAT IS DEFILEMENT?

What does the word "defilement" mean? Or what do we mean when we say something is defiled?

To be defiled is to be corrupted—that is, to be spiritually filthy. To be defiled is to be abominable to God. It is to be corrupted by sin and abhorred by God.

"To be defiled is to be spiritually filthy and polluted" (Zephaniah 3:1).

When a person is defiled, he becomes abominable to God, and the spirit of God departs from him. Marriage as an institution rooted in the word of God and His program for mankind can also be defiled.

God gave a specific instruction that *"marriage must be honorable and the bed undefiled" (Hebrews 13:4).*

> *So God gave a commandment and guided His people not to cause the fall of others through their dressing.*

Why is God so serious about this thing? It is because every individual among the human race represents a generation. God has invested so much on every individual for a generation. God does not create any man in a vacuum. Lives of human beings interrelate. Moses was created to deliver his generation, the children of Israel, from the bondage of Pharaoh. Jesus Christ was sent by God to deliver sinners through His death on the cross of Calvary. Jesus was born to rule as the King of kings and the Lord of lords *(John 18:37).*

When God invests so much in a person's life and the person allows himself to be corrupted, God severely punishes the person. The issue of defilement is therefore taken seriously by the Jews. The Bible says God will judge all whore mongers and adulterers and the fierce anger of the Lord God is awaiting every whore.

The Mystery of Sex

Let this be known to you, when a life is defiled that life and the seeds therein—that is, the generation yet unborn—will be defiled.

Judah, the son of Jacob, according to the program of God, was to bring forth the Messiah. It was the tribe of Judah that should hold the sceptre of God Almighty.

"The sceptre shall not depart from Judah, nor a lawgiver from between his feet until Shiloh come and to him shall the gathering of the people be" *(Genesis 49:10).*

The same Judah, under the influence of Satan, went forth to defile himself with a supposed harlot. The lady in question was not a harlot but his daughter-in-law, who had been promised in marriage with his youngest son after the death of Er and Onan, her first two husbands. As Judah did not fulfill the promise, Tamar went disguised as a harlot before Judah, and he went in to her in Genesis 38.

> *It has become very worrisome to see ladies in trousers walk shamelessly on our streets.*

This pollution might be the reason why Jesus did not come through the seed of Judah. To avoid pollution through the lineage of Judah, Jesus was conceived of the Holy Ghost.

The Almighty God takes the issue of defilement very seriously. Check out what the Bible says in *Ezekiel 16:20-21*:

"Moreover you have taken your sons and your daughters, whom you have borne to me and these have you sanctified

to them to be devoured. Is this of your whoredoms a small matter? That you have slain my children and delivered them to cause them to pass through the fire for them?"

The children the Lord is talking about here are the ones yet unborn. The Lord is saying they have been slain through whoredom and have been caused to pass through the fire, polluted and abhorred. And the Lord cried out in *Ezekiel 16:23*, *"Woe, woe! to you said the Lord."*

> A man who sees a beautiful woman and lusts after her commits adultery already in his heart.

Various Forms of Defilement:

Thoughts life can be defiled

In *Proverbs 23:7*, it is written, *"For as he thinks in his heart so is he."* Also *Proverbs 25:28* says, *"He that has no rule over his own spirit is like a city that is broken down and without walls."* Thoughts, if not controlled, can bring defilement to one's marriage and life.

Adultery starts in the heart. Once the thought of adultery enters one's heart, and it is meditated upon, as far as God is concerned that heart is already defiled. The person is already guilty of adultery before the Lord and His angels, even though he has not physically committed the act.

"You have heard that it was said by them of old time. You shall not commit adultery. But I say to you, that whosoever looks on a woman to lust after her has committed adultery with her already in his heart." Matthew 5:27-28).

This scripture says the mere thought of adultery makes one an adulterer.

A medical doctor, a born-again Christian, died suddenly. He expected to appear in Heaven. But he found himself in darkness, held and led by two personalities whose faces he couldn't see. He discovered that as they were going, there was heat, and the heat became hotter as they advanced in the journey. Suddenly, he heard a shout. "Stop!" Then a very beautiful creature queried, "Is it not written, 'No unclean thing shall enter into that place'?" And a voice answered from the throne of God Almighty: "Yes" The accuser then said, "This man is full of adultery of the heart. Therefore he cannot be allowed to enter." The Almighty responded, "Yes, it is true but look at the wife praying." At that point, the doctor saw his wife praying fervently over his lifeless body. And the Lord commanded that he should be taken back to life. And he came back to life, having seen many people dragged to hell fire.

If not for the sake of the wife, this man would have entered hell on account of adultery of the heart. He quickly abandoned his medical practice and went into preaching of the gospel, testifying about how God saved him from hell.

THE TONGUE CAN ALSO BRING DEFILEMENT

Many couples are fond of tongue lashing each other. At the slightest provocation, they will use their tongue to rail at people, especially at children and housemaids. This brings defilement to their life and marriage every day. Some people are even fond of cursing others at the slightest offense, bringing defilement into their life and the life of others.

> *The plan of the devil is to defile all women. Whether young, old, single or married; he desires to pollute and defile all.*

"How shall I curse whom God has not cursed or how can I defy whom the Lord has not defied" (Numbers 23:8).

The scripture says the tongue can defile people and their life.

"And the tongue is a fire, a world of iniquity, so is the tongue among our members that it defiles the whole body, and sets on fire the course of nature; and it is set on fire of hell" (James 3:6).

The power of the tongue has both life and death.

The tongue is referred to "as an unruly evil, full of deadly poison. Therewith bless we God, even the father and therewith curse we men which are made after the similitude of God" (James 3:8-9).

Life and marriage can be brought under a terrible defilement. We must learn to exercise control over our tongue.

Your Dressing can Defile you

Man, as I said earlier, is central in God's creation and program. God is the Holy God who commanded His people to be holy in other to remain in His presence. Anything God calls an abomination must be avoided seriously by anyone who intends to dwell in God's presence.

Unfortunately, many Christians treat the issue of dressing with levity. In fact, some people say dressing has nothing to do with the state of the heart and that the heart determines the position of an individual with the Lord God. Yes, it may be so, but God states clearly and expressly that our ways must not cause others to stumble.

> *Angels who gave themselves to fornication with strange flesh are the rebellious ones, not good and holy Angels.*

A good Christian must not cause the fall of others. So God gave a commandment and guided his people not to cause the fall of others through their dressing.

God was the first tailor in the entire universe, for God made a coat of skin for Adam and his wife, Eve, to cover their nakedness when sin and disobedience brought them shame and nakedness.

God wants every man and woman to cover their nakedness and be properly dressed. However, a lot of people have thrown decent dressing into the winds. Christian sisters dress almost naked when they go to church. They wear different garments, created through satanic influence, to expose certain sensuous parts of their body. Some of these garments are so tight on them that the curves and shapes of their body become obvious to their male counterparts whom they target to lure into sex with them. These are foundations for sinful sexual desires. *"As lust is conceived it will give birth to sin, and sin when is finished brings forth death" (James 1:15).*

When a married woman, a Christian sister, dresses sinfully, she brings defilement to her marital bed. It does not really matter whether the actual vice has been done or not. The Bible says adultery is already committed *(Matthew 5:28).*

> *Satan therefore employs the fallen nature of man to the maximum to prevent an average man from seeing the Lord.*

It has become very worrisome to see ladies in trousers walk shamelessly on our streets. In fact, of every ten ladies on the street, about six are in trousers. Unfortunately, the so-called Christians are not left out. This is a terrible phenomenon. It is worrisome.

But what does the Bible say concerning this?

"The woman shall not wear that which pertains to a man, neither shall a man put on a woman's garment, for all that do so are abomination to the Lord your God" (Deuteronomy 22:5).

What is the origin of this thing—woman wearing trousers? The origin can be traced back to Babylon where the worship of Baal started. It was the worshippers of Baal who dressed as such to offer sacrifice to their gods. Women would put on trousers meant for men, and men would put on a wrapper or skirt. But the God of Israel says it is an abomination to Him.

The Bible refers to this as strange apparel: *"And it shall come to pass in the day of the Lord's sacrifice that I will punish the Princes, and the King's children, and all such as are clothed in strange apparel" (Zephaniah 1:8).*

The Lord says He will punish the king's children. Who are the princes and the king's children? Christians, of course. Children of the King of kings and Lord of lords dressing in strange apparel are Christian ladies who dress sensuously. Every Christian must understand the action(s) he/she takes on his/her Christian journey and the consequences of such action(s).

> *The eyes can bring defilement to the heart and to the entire body, and set them against God.*

Christians are encouraged to follow the word of God and obey His commandments with all humility and meekness. We should allow the word of God to have a place in our heart.

"Let us lay apart all filthiness and superfluity of naughtiness and receive with meekness the engrafted word which is able to save our souls" (James 1:21).

DEFILEMENT THROUGH THE EYES

The eye is a gate through which the life of man could be defiled. The eye is the inroad to sinful desires. A man who sees a beautiful woman and lusts after her, commits adultery in his heart *(Matthew 5:28).*

The eyes of that man are the first instrument of unrighteousness. The woman may not even know that somebody sinfully desires her. From the human angle, one could say the woman is free from guilt, but spiritually, something has happened already which could even bring defilement to the woman.

> *Our God has given us His commandments, for us to escape from satanic plans for human destruction.*

Some eyes have penetrative power that spirits could enter. The evil spirits backing up the sinful desires in the life of lusting men could affect the actual deeds spiritually with the innocent woman they lust after.

Women having sex with known or unknown persons in a dream could have resulted from the lust that took place in the day. Any sexual activity in the dream is as real as the actual physical action. Therefore, once this is done, one could have been defiled. This is why women should be careful about the way they dress.

If a woman is so beautiful and she delights in dressing sensuously, such that heads of men begin to turn toward her, she is inviting serious trouble into her life.

To be quite honest, Satan hates women with a passion. This is because woman is central in the battle line drawn between God and the devil, as the seed of the woman shall bruise the head of the serpent *(Genesis 3:15).* And Satan knows that once the woman is polluted, corrupted, or defiled, her seed will not have any power to bruise his own head. So the plan of the devil is to defile all women, whether young, old, single or married; he desires to pollute all.

It should be noted that if a woman is adjudged beautiful to look at, she should be very prayerful and modest. Women must ensure that they cover their body very well. Why? It is because, apart from natural men, demons also seek to defile women.

> *All the rolling eyeballs, artificial eyelids, and eyelashes are all promoters of fornication and adultery.*

Let us check some scriptures on this issue.

In *1 Corinthians 11:6-12*, the Bible says, *"Man . . . is the glory and the image of God and the woman is the glory of man. . . . Neither was the man created for the woman, but the woman for the man. For this cause ought the woman to have power on her head because of the Angels."*

The angels we hear about could be holy angels or unholy angels (demons). Angels, both holy and unholy, still move around in the midst of children of men. Holy angels do good assignments while the unholy or evil ones perpetrate evil against the children of men. They carry out destructive assignments against the children of men as directed by Satan, their master.

Genesis 6:1-2, it says, "And it came to pass when men began to multiply on the face of the earth and daughters were born unto them. That the sons of God saw the daughters of men, that they were fair and they took them wives of all which thy chose."

Who are these sons of God? They are angels. As I said, angels can either be good and holy or evil and unholy.

In the book of *Jude 1:6-7*:

"And the angels which kept not their first estate, but left their own habitation, He has reserved in everlasting chains under darkness unto the judgment of the great day.

"Even as Sodom and Gomorrah, and the cities about them in like manner, giving themselves over to fornication, and going after strange flesh are set forth for an example, suffering the vengeance of eternal fire."

This scripture says some angels left their habitation and gave themselves to fornication, going about looking for strange flesh.

You can see from this scriptures that some angels that gave themselves to fornication with strange flesh are the rebellious ones, not good and holy angels.

However, they are still described as sons of God in *Genesis 6:7* and *Job 38:1*.

The plan of these evil angels is to pollute the daughters of men and destroy them.

If you are a woman, and you are lucky to read this book, you must mind the way you dress. If a woman is usually delighted to be sexually provocative in her mode of dressing, she is making the jobs of Satan easier in her life. She is like a fellow some powers want to roast for meal who wets her body with petrol and sits near the kiln. The agents of the devil will not ask for the opinion of the woman before they move in and start committing immorality with her. The woman has, knowingly or unknowingly, invited them into her life through her dressing. And the judgment of God is against the King's children who clothe themselves in strange apparels. *Zephaniah 1:8* has also given the satanic agents legal right over the life of the woman. All the provocative garments—body hugs, trousers, leggings, bare-backs, bare-fronts, and so on, in which ladies wriggle their body in public places and offices—are vehicles to torments and destruction. Ladies who dress sensuously are liable to satanic defilement, severe torments, and destruction await them in heaven.

THE EYES FULL OF ADULTERY

The enemy of our souls understands the spiritual components of our personality, their requirements, and what it takes to see the Lord. The enemy knows that no sinner can see the Lord. He therefore employs the fallen nature of man to the maximum to prevent an average man from seeing the Lord.

The Bible talks about the eye that is full of adultery. How can such eyes see the Lord? Let's consider this scripture: *"Having eyes full of adultery, that cannot cease from sin, beguiling unstable souls; an heart they have exercised with covetous practices, cursed children" (2 Peter 2:14).*

This scripture illustrates the state of an average man on the street beholding the vanities of the world- whorish women and vain material wealth. Once a man's eyes cannot cease from beholding these things, the entire spiritual body system will be defiled.

"The light of the body is the eye, if therefore your eye be single your whole body shall be full of light. But if your eye be evil [defiled] your whole body shall be full of darkness. If therefore the light that is in you be darkness [that is your eyes] how great is that darkness" (Matthew 6:22-23).

This scripture is saying that defiled eyes bring great defilement to the entire body. In fact, it throws darkness to the whole body. And when a life is in darkness, everything about that life will be full of darkness; the absence of light that will lead to all sorts of evil. The Bible says, *"The dark places of the earth are full of the habitations of cruelty" (Psalm 74:20).*

Darkness is the absence of light, the absence of the presence of God. It is, however, the presence of the devil and his agents.

The light of the body is the eye. If the eye is the light of the body, then one must ensure that darkness must not cover those eyes. That is to say, the eyes must not be defiled. Defilement of the eyes can cause defilement of the whole body.

The Bible says *if your right eye offends you, pluck it out, and cast it from you (Matthew 5:29).* This scripture is telling you not to allow your eye to offend you. Do not allow your eyes to defile your body, your marriage, and your home. It is better to pluck out those eyes, *for it is profitable for you that only one of your members should perish and not that your whole body should be cast into hell (Matthew 5:29).*

The eyes can bring defilement to the heart and to the entire body, and set them against God.

"Why does your heart carry you away? And what do your eyes wink at?" (Job 15:12).

"If my step has turned out of the way, and my heart walked after my eyes" (Job 31:7).

One should not allow one's heart to walk after the eyes. The eyes, if not controlled, have the power to carry one away from the path of holiness and righteousness. We therefore need to pray against our eyes beholding vanities and evils *(Psalm 119:37).*

There are lots of evil eyes in our environment. The devil has sent quite a number of whorish women with evil eyes to our streets. These women are assigned to hunt for the souls of men. They succeed in their destructive assignment with the aid of their eyes. Our God has, through the scriptures, given us His commandment for us to escape from satanic plans for human destruction.

"The Commandment is a lamp, and the law is light and reproof of instruction are the way of life. To keep you from the flattery of the tongue of a strange woman, from the

evil woman. Lust not after her beauty, neither let her take you with her eyelids" (Proverbs 6:23-25).

There are lots of women with serpents in their eyes and eyelids. They have captured many lives. Many men, sent by God to do great things for His kingdom, have been captured and reduced to a piece of bread with their eyelids. Samson was a great man of God, but a woman captured and destroyed his destiny.

"For by means of a whorish woman, a man is brought to a piece of bread and the adulteress will hunt for a precious life" (Proverbs 6:26).

A life can be captured and destroyed by sensuously powerful eyelids. Many husbands have been captured in various offices, restaurants, hotels, and even on the streets. And they have left their homes and found solace in the bosom of strange women. You legal wives whose husbands have been captured, the arm of the Lord will deliver your husband back to you, in Jesus name.

Job had to make a covenant with his eyes that he should not think upon a maid *(Job 31:1)*. Many Christians have to take this bold step and make a covenant with their eyes. When you know the truth, it is then it shall set you free. It is the truth you know that will set you free.

"If the eye that is in you be evil, how great is the darkness that is in you."

A lot of sisters have been unconsciously initiated into the dark world. Serpents have been programmed into their eyes. When they merely look at men, men will begin to shake and be thrown off balance. And they get whatever they want from any man of their choice.

If a sister continues in this satanic exploit, such a sister can never have a good marital relationship, let alone a stable home. Her demonic influence can only lead her to failure in every facet of life, including marriage, and it will ultimately lead to everlasting destruction.

"If your eye be evil, your whole body shall be full of darkness. If therefore the light that is in you be darkness, how great is that darkness" (Matthew 6:23).

Such sisters need immediate deliverance from the influence of Satan. They should pray serpents out of their eyes and lives. All the rolling eyeballs and made-up eyelids and eyelashes are all promoters of fornication and adultery. When married women still engage in such exploits, serious troubles and sudden destruction await them, as their death is imminent, and they are close to hell.

SAMPLE PRAYERS WHICH CHRISTIAN COUPLES MUST PRAY ALWAYS IN THEIR BEDROOM.
SCRIPTURES: PSALM 125

Aggressive Worship and Thanksgiving

Songs

Let the Fire of the Lord come down into this place. Let the fire of the Lord from heaven come down. Let the fire of the Lord come down.

Prayers

1. Every evil presence in our environment; what is your business here? Disappear by fire, in the name of Jesus.
2. Every evil eye delegated to watch over my bedroom, receive blindness, in the name of Jesus.
3. Every satanic mirror, within or outside, used to monitor my bedroom, shatter into pieces, in the name of Jesus.
4. You caldron of darkness with satanic water used to watch over my bedroom, break into pieces.
5. Every evil human spirit projected into my bedroom: die, die, die, in the name of Jesus.
6. You chariot of witchcraft en-route to my bedroom, be grounded and burn to ashes.
7. Holy Ghost fire envelope my bedroom now, in the name of Jesus.
8. Blood of Jesus, flow into my bedroom and cover every opening to the enemy, in the name of Jesus.
9. Chariot of fire, horses of fire of God of Elisha, surround my bedroom, in the name of Jesus.
10. Lord Jesus, accept our worship in body, soul and spirit, in the name of Jesus. Thank God, the Giver of life and good things,

CHAPTER FIVE

YOUR MARRIAGE
—THE SOUL OF YOUR LIFE

YOUR MARRIAGE—A GATE OF HEAVEN OR HELL?

What is a gate? A gate is an opening that is meant for a passage. It is a passage by which people gain access to a place. It is an opening that gives or denies people access to or out of a place. A gate can be open or shut.

Jacob went out on a journey toward Haran. And he stopped at a place and passed the night there because it was dark and unsafe to continue his journey. He took a stone and used it for his pillow, and lay down in that place to sleep. And he dreamt that a ladder was set up in the earth and the angels of God were ascending and descending on it. And the Lord stood above it and introduced Himself as the God of Abraham and Isaac, his fathers. And God spoke of His promise to Jacob and his seeds. As Jacob awoke out of his sleep, he said, "Surely, the Lord is in this place, and I know it not."

And he was afraid and said, "This is none other but the house of God, and this is the gate of heaven."

Abraham, the grandfather of Jacob, had raised an altar to the Lord in that same place, called Bethel. By the sacrifice he made to God, a gate was opened to the Lord. When Jacob found himself in that same place, the Lord appeared to him through the same gate, which he said was "the Lord's dwelling place, and a gate of heaven."

> *By the sacrifice Abraham made to God, a gate was opened to the Lord.*

When Adam and Eve were created, and the first marriage was instituted, God used to come and visit them at the cool of the day. Even now, God desires to visit his people to commune with them and to accept their daily sacrifice. The daily sacrifice can be offered to the Lord through worship to the Lord in spirit and in truth.

I said earlier that according to the scriptures, we do glorify God in our body—that is, our flesh. Sexual intercourse between a legally married couple can be a form of worship because the Lord is ever present with those who are His.

In a marriage, where an altar of daily sacrifice is raised to the Lord, a gate of heaven will be opened to the couple and their children. Angels of God are released to minister life and protection to them and to direct them in their daily activities (Hebrews 1:14).

A marriage where God dwells could be a gate of Heaven. However, that same marriage can be converted

The Mystery of Sex

to a gate of Hell, where evil spirits and demons from hell will dwell and inhabit.

If defilement is brought upon marriage through any form of sin, especially sexual sin, the Lord will promptly move away, and Satan, the author of sin, will enter. His influence will then be upon that marriage.

When a couple start engaging in any kind of sexual sin or perversion, an altar shall be raised to Satan and his host, and their marriage shall be converted to a gate of hell where evil spirits and demons inhabit.

Sin is an abomination to the Holy God, and once an abomination is present in a home, it will make the home devoid of the presence of God. The daily sacrifice shall be taken away, and the abomination that makes it desolate set up *(Daniel 12:11)*.

> *Husband and wife who sit down in the middle of the night watching immoral sexual/pornographic films, learning various forms of sexual styles are already in hell.*

In such a situation, many families will not remember to pray. The family altars will have broken down and all sorts of evil—fighting and watching of television and immoral films till midnight—will take over. Every activity in that home will be subject to satanic influence.

A husband and wife who sit down in the middle of the night and watch immoral sexual/pornographic films, learning various forms of sexual styles, are already in hell. The abomination that makes desolate is set up. The marriage of such a couple is already converted into a gate of hell, and evil spirits will be ascending and descending into their home from hell.

The Bible talks about a city that spiritually is called Sodom and Egypt. It is the place where our Lord was crucified *(Revelations 11:8)*.

The spirit of Sodom is the spirit behind sexual sins and various forms of perversion, and Egypt is a place of abomination. Jesus, the Son of God, was crucified for the sin of mankind. Any form of sinful behavior crucifies the Son of God afresh and put him to an open shame *(Hebrews 6:6)*.

> *The question now is, is your home a gate of heaven or a gate of the city of Sodom?*

When a home, through sexual sins, either adultery or any form of sexual perversions, is likened to a city of Sodom and Egypt, everybody in that home, including children, are appointed to drink from the cup of the wrath of God.

The question now is this: is your home a gate to heaven or a gate of the city of Sodom?

If abomination that makes desolate is present in your home, you will know through all kinds of filthy dreams—regular sex in the dreams and various forms of demonic activities in your dreams. But you can still do something: repent, cry to the Lord for mercy, and repair the altars of prayer that are broken down. Ask for the assistance of angels of God to eject every evil inhabitant from your home. Let fire of God and the Blood of Jesus build a wall around your home. Live a holy life.

Sex and Communication between Husband and Wife

Sexual communication breakdown has destroyed many marriages. It has sent quite a lot of couples onto a voyage of adultery and extramarital relationships, which ultimately have terminated joy in their home.

Sex is central or the main issue in marriage. It paves way for marital bliss. Marriage is the focal point in the union of God and man and the continuity of human race. Sex, therefore, is the heartbeat of the union between a man and a woman. Each partner needs the services of the other in this respect. This is why the Bible says it is better to marry than to burn *(1 Corinthians 7:9)*.

> *Partners must understand each other's sexual needs and provide such needs to give the desired satisfaction to each other.*

It is in marriage that solace can be found in the fulfillment of sexual desires—not in burning in adultery and fornication.

Sexual intercourse in marriage is a fundamental right of each partner that must not be denied.

The Bible says, *"Defraud you not one the other, except it be with consent for a time or with mutual agreement that they may give themselves to fasting and prayer and come together again, that Satan tempt you not for your incontinence"* *(1 Corinthians 7:5).*

Partners must understand each other's sexual needs and provide such needs to give the desired sexual satisfaction to each other.

There are some business executives who claim to have provided every comfort for their wives: money, food, clothes, and all the good things of life. Yet they deny their wives sexual satisfaction. Many of such executives will travel abroad for weeks, even months, leaving the poor woman in the cold at home. This has led so many wives into having sexual relationships, even with their drivers, cooks, houseboys, et cetera, downgrading their marital status.

> *The available house maid who ensures prompt meal at dinner now extends her duties and cares to the bedroom.*

When the mysterious sexual appetite comes over them, they could care less about the status of whoever is available at home to satisfy their sexual needs. Many husbands too have opened up the skirts of housemaids. In fact, some sophisticated housemaids have taken over the homes of many of their mistresses. They have usurped the position of the legal wives because Daddy is sexually starved for weeks, as the madam is always traveling on official duties. The available housemaid who ensures a prompt meal at dinner extends her duties and cares to the bedroom.

This communication breakdown in the bedroom has rendered many homes desolate.

Paul the Apostle encouraged the couples in the Lord to give each other due benevolence for the perfect union of the body.

The Mystery of Sex

"Let the husband render to the wife due benevolence and likewise also the wife to the husband. The wife has no power of her own body but the husband and likewise also the husband has not power of his own body, but the wife. Defraud you not one the other" (1 Corinthians 7:3-5).

This scripture is saying that the body of the woman belongs to the husband. It has become the property of the man. Likewise, the body of the man belongs to the woman. It has equally become the property of the woman. If the woman demands for sex in that marriage, it is her legal right to which the man has no power to say no, and vice versa.

Quite a lot of women even use sex to manipulate their husband. When they know that the man has a visible appetite for it, they try to deny him his right, giving some inglorious conditions before they cooperate with him. This kind of action is nothing but witchcraft manipulation. It can provoke God to anger against such women.

> *God is the author of marriage, and that same God does not want anything to jeopardise the good thing he has instituted.*

Some men also, having been stressed up in their daily activities, especially in their work place, also deny their wives.

If the woman, out of frustration and under satanic influence, goes into adultery, the man will not be guiltless, especially when the woman is caught in the act and the man decides to forsake her. The Bible says *the man causes her to commit adultery (Matthew 5:32).*

Couples should not allow themselves to be used by Satan against each other.

It is important to note this: some people are never satisfied with sex. They make their partners miserable, as their demands are insatiable. If anyone is in this condition, the best thing to do is to go for deliverance. The spirit behind this action will be pulled out of their lives. This can only be done through prayer. Let the couple pray for each other.

> *Communication between husband and wife, especially in bed, must not be broken down.*

Some ministers of God claim to engage in the service of the Lord and get so deeply involved in church activities that they neglect the home front. Such ministers know that God may not accept their services.

The home is very important and must not be neglected. God is the author of marriage. That same God would not want anything to jeopardize the good thing He has instituted. God, through Moses, commanded the children of Israel that *"when a man has taken a new wife, he shall not go out to war, neither shall he be charged with any business; but he shall be free at home one year and shall cheer up his wife which he has taken"* (Deuteronomy 24:5).

Through this scripture, we can understand the importance God attributes to a good relationship between husband and wife. The man must cheer up his wife. The woman must not be left alone. The man must make her happy. If by any means the man is involved

The Mystery of Sex

in a spiritual assignment, it must be a joint decision to abstain from sex, following a mutual understanding of the need to do so. If a man decides to go into fasting and prayer, the wife must agree with him. Likewise the husband when the wife wants to engage in prayer and fasting.

Women married to unbelievers must be very careful in this regard. When such women are into fasting and prayer and their husbands demand sex, they must not deny them their right if they fail to reason with them. Communication between husband and wife, especially in bed, must not be broken down. It is very important

THE HONEYMOON AFTER THE WEDDING:

THE FIRST TIME EXPERIENCE

A lot of couples look forward to this day with excitement. Many travel far to a quiet place with a

> *Do you know that some human personalities could engage in astral travels to attack new couples on their first day of marriage?*

good intention to rest after the stress of their engagement and wedding ceremonies. Only very few people understand the spiritual contractual operation that is bound to take place the very first day of their marital union. As a result of this serious spiritual ignorance, the devil waits for this day in many marriages to launch his missiles against many ignorant couples. All the sequential marital problems, such as barrenness, sickness, poverty, marital discord, untimely death, et cetera, start that very day.

Quite a number of Christian couples are in the dark about events that take place inside the room they find themselves. The Bible says we should not be ignorant of the devices of the devil.

This book should be an eye opener to many who desire freedom and want to live in dominion. The first thing the devil does is to manipulate people into marrying wrong partners. If the devil succeeds in this respect, he knows he would be in total control of that marriage. However, if he fails and the couple are able to find the right partners, he moves into another realm of attack, which would be targeted at the couple. This is usually done on the first day of the wedding.

> *... prepare against every possible onslaught of Satan and his host before, during and after. .. wedding; especially on the wedding day*

This is why pre-marital sex is very dangerous and risky for couples, even when the right partners are able to locate themselves.

With a singular pre-marital sexual experience, a marriage could have been handed over to Satan.

There was a movie I watched sometimes ago. The new couple was in their closet. The wife was very happy, trying to undress for the first time before her husband, who watched her with keen interest. As the man tried to grab her from behind, her spiritual husband appeared, though they did not see him. He shot a wicked arrow at the innocent husband who died instantly. The woman cried for her joy was converted to sorrow.

A couple got married, and for a period of over ten years, they had no issue. Many tests were carried out on them. The woman had no problem but the man, according to medical reports, had a low sperm count. They tried various medical means, but there was no improvement. At that level, they started to pray. After serious prayers, there was a revelation that the first day he had sex with his wife, a spiritual personality was right inside the room with them. It was also revealed to them that the fellow collected the man's sperm in a calabash and disappeared with it to an altar, where it was rendered ineffective.

Do you know that some human personalities could engage in astral travels to attack new couples on their first day of marriage?

Some witches had confessed to this satanic spiritual practice. Many satanic mothers-in-law launch their attacks on their prey on the wedding day.

Let me say this: Sexual intercourse is both physical and spiritual as it involves the presence of some spiritual personalities, apart from the couple. The spiritual personality could either be the angel of God who guides the children of God and brings blessings upon the exercise or the demons of the devil, which attack and bring curses upon the exercise.

There is no neutral ground; either of them must be present. Through sex, an altar is either raised to the Lord or to the devil, depending on the circumstance surrounding the exercise.

The Bible says, *"My people are destroyed for lack of knowledge" (Hosea 4:6)*. Children of God must not be ignorant of the devil's devices. Rather, they must prepare against every possible onslaught from Satan and his host before, during, and after the wedding, especially on the wedding day.

The wise couple would, throughout the first few days of their union, engage in serious prayers with fasting. If it would be possible, they must clear all the debris of the past that may have form sediments in their lives. Such debris could be youthful sins, inherited sins, evil dedication, family bondage, et cetera. All these legal footholds of Satan must be removed through deliverance prayers so that the couple will start a new life and a new family with a clean slate.

Any time a couple want to come together in bed, they must wholeheartedly praise and worship God and pray fervently to bring down the presence of God and His fire. They must pray to build a wall around them so that any spiritual satanic personality around will not be able to get close to them.

This is a great secret that many do not know. Rather than engaging in any funfair or carnally controlled honeymoon, it is better for a new couple to climb the mountain of power in God. It is also good for the couple to know the spiritual state of each other. At these dangerous hours of the last days, it will amount to foolishness for any man or woman to engage in marital black market.

CHAPTER SIX

COMMON SEXUAL PERVERSIONS AMONG LEGALLY MARRIED COUPLES

I was in a place with a friend sometimes ago, and a discourse came up about ladies who snatch husbands from their wives. A sister said that the weapons of husband snatchers are, basically, various sexual styles and capabilities that give satisfaction the husbands may not derive from their wives. And when the captured husband "tastes" the innovative sexual options, different from the usual, he will practically abandon the "bed" at home. The sister went further that the only way to prevent strange women from snatching men from their legal wives is for the wives to engage in watching pornographic films to enable them satisfy their husbands with the various styles in the pornographic films and literatures.

This, certainly, is a satanic solution that will bring no positive result. It will only introduce more problems into the marriage. If a Christian attempts this prescription because of the fear of her unbelieving husband being snatched away from her, she will enter into greater troubles, both with God and the devil.

There is no doubt, various sexual perversions among couples, even Christian couples, originate from the desire to give optimum satisfaction to each other. The satisfaction derivable from demonic options is no match to the trouble and confusion that will follow, which could scatter the home and worsen the couple's spiritual experience.

I have said earlier that sexual intercourse is both physical and spiritual. In consideration of the spiritual state, altars, gates, and doors are opened to some unseen personalities, who may not even be visible to the couple in the very act.

These unseen personalities influence the satanic control of the lives of the couple and their children. They also curse the couple performing the sexual act outside the heavenly prescription. And immediately they issue curses on the couple, some spirit beings will swing into action to enforce the curses upon the couple, their children, and their generation.

> *Quite a lot of women would be accused of murder when they appear at the judgement seat of God; for they have killed many seeds with their mouth.*

Various forms of Sexual Perversion

i. Oral Sex

Oral sex is a situation where the woman uses her mouth in lieu of her sexual organ to give the man sexual pleasure. Many human seeds, with life in them, have been swallowed up by whorish women.

The Bible says, *"A seed shall serve him; it shall be accounted to the Lord for a generation" (Psalm 22:30).*

Many seeds that would have come to the world and would probably have gendered into generations, fulfilling Gods purpose have been wasted on the altar of oral sex.

Abraham, the father of nations, was a seed in the loins of Terah, his father. Imagine Abraham, while he was yet a seed, being wasted during oral sex. How would he have fulfilled that purpose? God does not purpose the mouth of a woman for sexual intercourse. Quite a lot of women will be accused of murder when they appear at the judgment seat of God, for they have killed many seeds with their mouth. And the man who gave his seed out to a strange woman shall not be innocent.

> *There is no doubt, various sexual perversions among couples, even Christian couples, originate from the desire to give optimum satisfaction to each other.*

"And I will set my face against that man, and will cut him off from among his people, because he has given of his seed to Molech" (Leviticus 20:3).

The practice of oral sex attracts very stiff judgment from the Lord. Therefore, anyone who does it must repent fast before it is too late.

ii. ANAL SEX

Some couples engage in an unnecessary sexual practice, Anal sex—an act whereby a man inserts his sexual organ in the anus of his partner. Sounds strange! Yet it happens, even among legally married couples.

Beloved, men get into this shameful affair of reading romantic novels and pornographic journals and of watching pornographic films. These practices gets them sexually aroused. As a result, they are desirous of sex, willing to experiment all that they have read or watched, for maximum sexual pleasures. Once they find the experimentation pleasurable, they stick to it and find it difficult to stop. But God does not purpose the anus of anybody, either man or woman, for sex.

> *Many husbands have been snatched, many souls have been traded out into the kingdom of Satan on the altar of sex.*

I still wonder about the involvement of couples in this dirty act. There is no doubt about the influence of an unclean spirit being the power behind this persuasive sexual indulgence. No man or woman filled with Holy Spirit of God would engage in such an immorality. It is definitely the doctrine of the devils. And when it becomes habitual, the journey toward unexpected and unpalatable experience is also set.

The Bible says, "Even their women did change natural use into that which is against nature. And likewise also the men leaving the natural use of the woman in their lust" *(Romans 1:26-27)*.

Sexual distortion as manifested in anal sex is a vile affection. It is unacceptable to God. It is abhorred to nature and the entire creations. Unfortunately, some Christian couples do indulge in this sexual recklessness, ignorant of its implications.

The body of man has nine opening: eyes—two; ears—two; mouth—one; nose—two; and anus—one. Each of the openings has its specific purposes. The body of man does not belong to him but to the Creator of the body. The misuse of any of these openings would breakdown the spiritual defense of the abuser. This is why the enemy of the soul of man always provokes or deceives man into error through negative doctrine inspired by seducing spirits *(I Timothy 4:1)*,

> *Many human seeds, with life in them, have been swallowed up by whorish women.*

If a man gets involved in such an immorality, he finds it hard to quit, and gradually his conscience becomes sealed with iron—abnormal till the time judgment is set.

Immediate repentance is the only antidote for averting god's wrath and heavy judgment. Spiritually, when defense system of a life is broken down, plagues of Egypt will bombard and infiltrate that life.

These plagues could come in various forms including terrible sickness that defile medications, different forms of affliction, and steady and gradual destruction. Oral or anal sex is a serious abuse of the body, which

The Mystery of Sex

a true child of God must resist, even if unregenerated partner demands it. It must be vehemently resisted.

HAVING SEX DURING MENSTRUATION

Some people find it difficult to control their sexual urge when it comes upon them. Therefore, they engage in sex even when the woman's menstrual circle is on. This is a very dirty act in the physical; it is terrible, filthy, and bad in the spiritual.

It does not really matter whether the woman is your wife or not. God gave a standing commandment, forbidding this practice among His children.

"Thou shall not approach unto a woman to uncover her nakedness as long as she is put apart for her uncleanness" (Leviticus 18:19).

> *Many women would be accused of murder when they appear at the judgement seat of God; for they have killed many seeds with their mouths.*

And another scripture says, "And if a man shall lie with a woman having her sickness and shall uncover her nakedness, he has discovered her fountain and she has uncovered the fountain of her blood and both of them shall be cut off from among their people" (Leviticus 20:18).

This second scripture says the man has discovered the source of the life of the woman, and the woman too has uncovered or opened up the source of her life.

The Bible says "life is in the blood." If a woman opens up her life to an enemy (such as occultic men that delight in drinking blood) through sex during her menstrual period, anything evil could happen to her. Arrows could be fired at her and sickness like issue of blood could come in to her. It is a very serious matter.

And the man involved could get himself defiled, bringing the sanctuary of the Lord, which is his body, into filthy and terrible state of defilement. It is very unfortunate that quite a lot of people involve themselves in this spiritual and sexual crime against their bodies, soul, and spirit.

> *Sleeping with a woman during her menstruation is a perversion of sexual gifts.*

Let's consider another scripture: *"If a man be just, and do that which is lawful and right. And has not eaten upon the mountain, neither has lifted up his eyes to the idols of the house of Israel, neither has defiled his neighbors wife, neither has come near to a menstruous woman" (Ezekiel 18:5-6).*

According to this scripture, coming near a menstruating woman is an act that is seen as disobedience to God. Sleeping with a woman during her menstruation is a perversion of sexual gifts.

And David sent messengers and took her, and she came in to him and he lay with her *"for she was purified from her uncleanness" (2 Samuel 11:4).*

According to this scripture, if that woman was not purified from her uncleanness—that is, if her menstrual circle was on as at that time—David might not

The Mystery of Sex

have gone ahead and committed sexual immorality with her.

Sleeping with a woman during her menstruation is a perversion of sexual act. Anyone who has ever engaged in it needs serious spiritual purification and purging. It takes only the Blood of Jesus for that life to be made whole and clean again.

The Bible says, *"Defile not you yourselves in any of these things; for in all these the nations are defiled which I cast out before you. And the land is defiled; therefore I do visit the iniquity thereof upon it and the land itself vomited out her inhabitants.*

> "Defile not you yourselves in any of these things; for in all these the nations are defiled which I cast out before you".

"Ye shall therefore keep my statutes and my judgements and shall not commit any of these abominations, neither any of your own nation, nor any stranger that sojourneth among you. For all these abomination have the men of the Land done, which were before you and the land is defiled.

"That the land spue not you out also, when ye defile it as it spued out the nation's that were before you. For whosoever shall commit any of this abominations, even the souls that commit them shall be cut off among their people. Therefore shall ye keep mine ordinance, that ye commit not any one these abominable customs which were committed before you and that ye defile not yourselves there in. I am the Lord your God" (Leviticus 18:24-30).

Sam Kunle-Oluwatobi

The word of God says whosoever is wise will observe these things, even they shall understand the loving kindness of the Lord *(Psalm 107:43)*.

It is now very clear that common abominable sexual acts and customs bring great defilement on the land on which we dwell. And the land spews out those who bring defilement upon it. This therefore attests to the fact that violence, crime, and untimely death are common in our land and environment because nations and families have been sold out through whoredom and witchcraft *(Nahum 3:4)*.

CHAPTER SEVEN

YOUR VIRGINITY AND YOUR DESTINY

"But if this thing be true, and the tokens of virginity be not found for the damsel; Then they shall bring out the damsel to the door of her father's house, and the men of her city shall stone her with stones that she die" (Deuteronomy 22:20-21).

When we talk of virginity, a lot of people cast their minds on sisters alone, not on brothers. People believe that the virtue of keeping virginity intact till marriage is only demanded from sisters.

Many brothers, through ignorance, have slaughtered their own destinies on the altar of careless sex. They have sold out everything God created in them to immorality. Their original birthright has been sold to power of darkness on the altar of youthful sex. Therefore, many kings and rulers have been reduced to servants. Employers of labor are now demoted to employees. People who are supposed to give instructions are now taking instructions from those who are lower than them.

The words in *Ecclesiastes 10:7* have come to reality in many lives: "I have seen servants upon horse and prince's walking as servants upon the earth." This is a great tragedy taking place in the midst of children of men.

Let us consider the scriptural insights into this: *"Lest there be any fornicator or profane person as Esau who for one morsel of meat sold his birthright. For ye know how that afterward when he would have inherited the blessing he was rejected; for he found no place of repentance though he sought it carefully with tears."* Esau sold his birthright for food.

A lot of brothers are roaming about the streets today because they have sold out their birthright on the altar of five minutes of sex while they were in schools. Today, their lives have been cast down because all their virtues have been sold out.

A fornicator or a profane person will sell out his or her entire life, though ignorantly, as a result of five minutes of sexual pleasure. What a terrible bargain!

> *A fornicator or a profane person would sell out his or her entire life, though ignorantly, as a result of five minutes' sexual pleasure. What a terrible bargain!*

WHAT IS VIRGINITY?

Virginity is taken from the word virgin. The word virgin means uncultivated, untouched, fresh, naturally kept intact, chaste, not yet known, pure, not yet bruised, not yet violated, has not been visited upon, has not been treaded upon, the natural seal of protection is intact, not ruptured, the "teat of virginity" is still there intact; and finally, the state of being a virgin.

The Mystery of Sex

There is a physical and spiritual seal of protection over the inner structure of both male and female. In a female, the physical seal is visible, but it is not visible in a male. The foreskin that is visible in male, which must be removed, does not constitute virginity.

The state of virginity is not physical in male. In female, the teat of virginity constitutes the natural zeal of protection over the inner structure; and once it is bruised or violated, the status of a virgin or maiden is lost, and it is believed the lady or maid has been visited upon or devirgined.

When the teat of virginity, which constitutes the physical seal, is bruised or ruptured, blood will come out, and the bedspread that receives the blood's stain becomes the *"token of virginity"* *(Deuteronomy 22:17)*.

> *Your virginity therefore is the coats of skin or seal of protection that is used to clothe every man or woman born into this world.*

When a maid is betrothed to a man, the husband is expected to find the maid a virgin and to give a positive report of a state of pureness and uncultivatedness. Usually, the love of the man for the new wife would increase when the new wife was found to be a virgin. But if the token of virginity was not found, the wife could be sentenced to death. This was the practice among the Jews in those days. They believed the lady must have played whoredom in her father's house *(Deuteronomy 22:21)*.

Among the old Yoruba nations, if the token of virginity was found, the wife had brought great glory and honor to her father, and even her entire family. On the contrary, she had brought shame, dishonor to her father and her family. And culturally, the maid and her father would be made to pass through some rituals usually associated with shame, disgrace, and dishonor.

The state of virginity is important to be kept, culturally and scripturally.

In a male, there is no means by which the state of pureness or virginity can be discovered; however, terrible things can happen to any young man who involves himself in a pre-marital sexual adventure or relationship. When Adam and Eve fell into the sin of disobedience, they found themselves naked, and the glory of God created with them was automatically replaced with shame, for sins always bring shame and nakedness. And they went and hid themselves from the presence of the Lord. They could not stand boldly before the Lord, for the glory of God had departed from them. But God, through his abundance of mercies, did not leave Adam and his wife naked. God knew that leaving them naked was dangerous and that all good things He had created with them which were, as a result of their sin, opened to spiritual aggressors and robbers, could be stolen. God therefore clothed them with coats of skin.

> *For anyone to keep his or her virginity is to keep the destiny.*

"To Adam also and to his wife did the Lord God make coats of skin and clothed them" (Genesis 3:21). The coat

of skin was a seal of protection upon Adam and his wife. And every individual that is born of flesh and blood is always with this seal of protection. The only operation that can rupture this seal is sexual intercourse. And once that seal is ruptured, every good thing in that life can be stolen, especially when the sexual partner is an agent of darkness, and the sexual act is done in sin. This is why the Bible refers to sex as "having knowledge of" or "carnal knowledge" or "uncovering the nakedness of" *(Genesis 4:1, Leviticus 18:6).*

Your virginity therefore is the coat of skin that is used to clothe every man or woman born into this world. It is a seal, of covering the nakedness of every man or woman.

One occultic man was looking for money. It is clear that occultic people use blood of human beings to make money.

> *All the good things packaged together for a glorious destiny could be lost on account of fornication.*

Being a very decent man, he would not accept any crude and indecent approach to his demonic undertakings. He rejected all the crude options given to him, like sleeping in a cemetery for days, buying a live goat in the market place, killing either his wife or any of his children, et cetera. At last, he chose to have sex with a virgin whose life was a gold mine and who was loaded with virtues.

The man made that choice, believing that it was stress free. Now the question is: what will happen to the unfortunate girl when the money starts coming in? Her life will be converted into a dustbin.

Many occultic men are still looking for virgins every day, to steal their virtues. There are many sugar mummies looking for young blood to sleep with. Sexual looseness is practically a program of self-destruction. For anyone to keep his or her virginity is to keep the destiny.

Many destinies have been destroyed on the altar of sex. Sex has become a graveyard of many nobles, whose lives were supposed to be glorious. All the good things packaged together for a glorious destiny could be lost on account of fornication.

> *Prostitution or whoredom is the mother of wickedness.*

A MAID WHO REMAINS A VIRGIN RECEIVES THE FAVOR OF GOD AND MAN

God favors all who obey his commandments and walk in His words, law, and statutes. Mary, the virgin, who was espoused to Joseph of the house of David, found favor with God. She was singled out among other damsels to bring forth the Savior of the world. God is still looking and searching for beautiful and obedient sisters who shall not defile themselves but shall remain virgins in their maiden years. God is greatly interested in them to be espoused to His own children and to bring forth His prophets.

God always gives specific instructions to His priests and prophets not to marry a whore or a woman put away by her husband *(Leviticus 21:7).*

The Mystery of Sex

"And he shall take a wife in her virginity. A widow, or a divorcee woman or profane, or an harlot these shall he not take, but he shall take a VIRGIN of his own people to wife" (Leviticus 21:13-14).

There are many sisters who are crying day and night for a husband, and there seems to be no hope. In fact, many of them sometimes threaten to go back to the world. They do blame God for unanswered prayers. The truth of the matter is that, they have never departed from the world. Many are living a reckless sexual life. As far as Heaven is concerned, they are defiled, and nothing but harlots in the sight of God and His angels. God will never recommend a harlot to His own children or prophets. This is because the prophets and children of God are holy to Him.

> *Unfortunately, many sisters don't consider their virginity status as very important to be kept. They lose their virginity cheaply.*

According to the program of God, many of these sisters have wasted their lives and destinies through whoredom. Many of them have aborted their seeds who ought to bruise the head of the serpents troubling their immediate environment *(Genesis 3:15).*

Check out the lives of the mothers of God's generals: apostles and prophets making waves for God in His Kingdom, causing serious troubles in the camp of the enemy. You would discover that they did not live a reckless sexual life in their maiden years. That was why God gave them such glorious children.

Many women are already condemned, awaiting execution by God and His angels for their immoral lives during their maiden years.

> ... and they bruised the breast of her virginity and poured their whoredom upon her.

A sister was led into immorality by her friends who deceived her to believe that her breast would remain small unless she had regular sex. Eventually this sister had a boyfriend and indulged in immorality in her secondary school days. Later, she was impregnated three times and aborted the three pregnancies.

After her education, she became born again and got married, but there was no issue for years.

The destiny of this sister was to bring forth three glorious men who would shake the entire world Unfortunately, all these three men were aborted in her youth.

Now a woman, after serious prayers one night, she had a dream: she saw three big men, with their aides carrying briefcases behind them. When she was told that the three big men were her children, she was happy. She was later ushered in to where the three men were. There she found a sword in her hand. One after the other, she cut off the heads of these three men. Then she woke up and was greatly troubled about the dream. The Holy Spirit then reminded her of the three pregnancies she had previously aborted.

The Mystery of Sex

Whoredom in days of one's youth is not a small matter. God reserves a terrible wrath against all whores. The Bibles says, "All whore mongers shall be judged" *(Hebrews 13:4)*. Prostitution or whoredom is the mother of wickedness. When practiced, the land is defiled and full of wickedness *(Leviticus 19:29)*. Imagine the wickedness of that sister who cut off the heads of her three glorious children whom God had determined to use to positively affect the entire world. The sister cut off the heads of her three children in wickedness and whoredom. Could one imagine Mary, the mother of Jesus, caught in whoredom? It's unimaginable. It would have been terribly sad for her, for the wrath of God rather than God's favor would have visited her.

> *And they shall deal with you hatefully and shall take away all your labour, and shall leave you naked and bare.*

We appreciate the grace of God upon her, that she lived a holy life, remained a virgin in her days, and fulfilled her destiny in bringing forth the Savior of the whole world—the man Jesus Christ of Nazareth.

Unfortunately, many sisters don't consider their virginity status very important. They lose their virginity cheaply and get married in their whorish state.

The Bible talks about tokens of virginity that must be found in the life of a damsel betrothed for marriage. And if it is not found, a death sentence awaits such a damsel. Consider this scriptural insights;

"But if this thing be true and the tokens of virginity be not found for the damsel; then they shall bring out the damsel to the door of her father's house and men of her father's house and men of her city shall stone her with stones that she die, because she hath wrought folly in Israel, to play whore in her father's house, so that thou put evil away from among you" (Deuteronomy 22:20-21).

> The seed of God that is in you is created with you for the fulfilment of God's purpose and plan. When that seed which is in you, either man or woman, is poured out in whoredom, you are seen as a murderer.

So playing whore as a maid attracts severe punishment from the Lord. Let us consider those who played whore in their father's house in the scriptures.

In *Ezekiel 23*, the Bible talks about two women, daughters of one mother, who committed whoredom in their youth.

And they committed whoredom in their youth; there were their breasts pressed and there they bruised the teats of their virginity. These women that committed whoredoms in their youth were daughters of Israel whose names were Aholah the elder, and Aholibah her younger sister Aholah gave birth to Samaria while Aholibah had Jerusalem.

These two women committed whoredom with all them that were chosen men of Assyria, and with all as whom she doted with all their idols she defiled herself.

The Mystery of Sex

Neither left she her whoredom brought from Egypt, for in her youth they lay with her, and they bruised the breast of her virginity and poured their whoredom upon her. Wherefore I have delivered her unto the hand of her lovers, with the hand of the Assyrian upon she doted.

These discovered her nakedness, They took her sons and her daughters and slew her with the sword and she became famous among women; for they had executed judgement upon her.

And when her sister Aholibah saw this, she was more corrupt in her inordinate love than she and in her whoredoms, more than her sister in her whoredoms. She doted upon the Assyrians, her neighbour, captains and rulers, clothed most generously, horsemen riding upon horses, all of them desirable young men.

Then I saw that she was defiled that they took both one way. And that she increased her whoredoms; for when she saw men portrayed upon the wall, the images of Chaldeans portrayed with vermilion

And as soon as she saw them with her eyes, she doted upon them and sent messengers unto them into Chaldea.

And the Babylonians came to her into the bed of love, and they defiled her with their whoredom and she was polluted with them and her mind was alienated from them.

So she discovered her whoredoms and discovered her nakedness, then my mind was alienated from her like my mind was alienated from her sister. Yet she multiplied her whoredoms, in calling to remembrance the days of her youth, wherein she had played the harlot in the land of Egypt. For she doted upon their parmous whose flesh is a flesh of asses and whose issue is like the issue of horses.

Thus thou calledst to remembrance the lewdness of thy youth, in bruising thy teats by the Egyptians for the paps of thy youth.

Therefore O Aholibah thus said the Lord God.

Behold I will raise upon thy lovers against thee, from whom thy mind is alienated and I will bring them against thee as every side.

For thus said the Lord God, I will deliver thee into the hand of them whom thou hatest, into the hand of them whom thy mind is alienated. And they shall deal with thee hatefully and shall take away all thy labour, and shall leave thee naked and bare, and the nakedness of thy whoredoms shall be discovered both thy lewdness and thy whoredoms.

I will do these things into thee because thou hast gone awhoring after the heathen and because thou art polluted with their idols.

Verse 33: Thou shall be filled with drunkenness and sorrow, with the cup of astonishment and desolation verse 46: For thus saith the Lord God. I will bring up a company upon them and will give them to be removed and spoiled.

And the company shall stone them with stones and dispatch them with their swords, they shall slay their sons and their daughters and burn up their houses with fire.

Thus will I cause lewdness to cease in the land, that all women may be taught not to do after your lewdness. And they shall recompense your lewdness upon you, and ye shall bear the sins of your idols and ye shall know that I am the Lord God (Ezekiel 23:3-49).

The Mystery of Sex

In consideration of this passage, it's very clear that whoredom is a terrible sin before God and His angels, and the fury of the Lord's anger is awaiting every whore monger.

The power and the spirit behind whoredom is still the spirit of Babylon that stands against anything that is of God Almighty. When children of God commit whoredom with the heathen, it provokes God to anger, for our God is a jealous God and a consuming Fire.

> *Keeping your virginity till marriage is keeping your life time destiny. It must be guided with all determination, and with utmost care.*

The seed of God that is in you is created with you for the fulfillment of God's purpose and plan. When that seed which is in you is poured out in whoredom, you (whether man or woman) are seen as a murderer.

"Moreover you have taken your sons and your daughters whom you have borne to me, and these have you sacrificed to them to be devoured. Is this your whoredoms a small matter?" (Ezekiel 16:20).

Those seeds that shall serve the Lord, which must have been sacrificed on the bed of fornication *(Psalm 22:30)* make your case a serious matter before the Lord God.

A lot of sisters are going through hell in their marriage today. Their husbands have become their enemies.

They try every means possible to please them, but they would not be impressed by their good deeds.

This is why the Lord is saying, *"They shall deal with you hatefully, and shall take away all your labour, and shall leave you naked and bare" (Ezekiel 23:29).*

And this scripture is fulfilled in many marriages today, because such marriages were established on the foundation of whoredom with the heathen and the Babylonians.

Sisters in the Lord should have a proper understanding of this thing and keep themselves pure. The most powerful force behind whoredom is the power that sits upon many waters; which the Bible called the great whore *(Revelations 17:1).* It is this power that is also called *MOTHER OF HARLOT AND ABOMINATION OF THE EARTH" (Revelations 17:5).*

This power always catches her agents at tender ages, teen years. The power casts demonic influence on the innocent girls at teenage years, when they are yet virgins.

All the indecent modes of dressing, prevalent in our society among ladies, are the strategies of this evil power. When girls are caught in this indecent act, they are initiated, and the evil influence of that power takes over their lives.

Parents in the Lord must understand these things and work hard to prevent their children from getting into the trap of this great whore.

Keeping your virginity till marriage is keeping your lifetime destiny. It must be guided with all determination and utmost care.

CHAPTER EIGHT
SPIRIT HUSBANDS AND SPIRIT WIVES

The concept of spirit husband and spirit wives is very strange to many people, especially the so-called Christians. And the devil has hidden the reality of this concept from people. He has by doing so succeeded in destroying many lives and marriages.

A lot of people are going through pains of barrenness, late marriage, poverty, strange sickness, et cetera, and they have not unraveled the mystery of their long suffering. Simple prayers against spirit husbands and wives would have brought succor and relief to them, and the joy and peace which hitherto have eluded them for years would have been promptly restored to them, had they known this fact—the reality of spirit husbands and wives.

Who is a spirit husband or wife? Before we can throw light on who the spirit husband or wife is, it is important for us to remind ourselves what makes a human personality.

A human personality is a spirit being living in a body and having a soul. This means, as you are reading this book, you are a spirit being, living in a body and having a soul. Your soul is your consciousness of yourself, environment, God, and anything you believe in. It is the awareness of your existence, that which makes you aware of who you are, your character and your intellect, which is your soul.

> *It is also important to note that the spirit beings do not die. They are eternally existent.*

It is also important to note that the spirit beings do not die. They are eternally existent.

This means that before you were born into this world, God knew you *(Jeremiah 1:5)*. And you had existed, even though you were not conscious of your existence then. And that even after death, you will still exist either with God or with the devil.

So technically, human spiritual personality doesn't die. They are eternally existent. This is real and true altogether. Whether you believe it or not, your opinion regarding this does not matter.

Having established the fact that human personalities are spirits, spirits husbands and wives are spirit beings, operating in the spiritual realm. They see humans as their peers since human beings are also spirit beings.

It is also important to note that God Himself is a Spirit *(John 4:24)*.

Since God is a spirit, He too extends His will and wish toward man through their spirits. The Bible says

The Mystery of Sex

the spirit of man is the candle of the Lord *(Proverbs 20:27)*.

Furthermore, Satan and his cohorts too are spiritual personalities. They too are spirits. The enemies of God and man consist not in the flesh and blood. (Remember, man is flesh and blood, having spirits inside the body.)

The Bible says we should *"put on the whole armour of God, to be able to stand against the wiles of the devil. For we wrestle not or fight not against flesh and blood, but against principalities against powers, against the rulers of darkness of this world, against spiritual wickedness in high places"* *(Ephesians 6:11-12).*

> *Satan is the driving force behind every form of worship that is demanded by force.*

God is a spirit, man is a spirit, and the devil too is a spirit. In the spiritual realm, there are only two camps, The camp of God, which represents light, and the camp of Satan or the devil, which represents darkness.

Man can move or operate in either of the camps. Man can operate with God or with the devil.

There is a serious battle over man between God and the devil. However, God is more supreme and powerful than the devil, but the wish or the will of man determines where he belongs.

God has already given the free will to mankind. God does not force His will on anyone. He wants all to exercise that will according to their personal desires and judgment.

Satan, however, through his wiles, tries to deceive man and to possibly enforce his will upon him, knowing full well the ignorance and frail nature of man.

Satan demands love, worship, loyalty, followership et cetera, from men. Sometimes he capitalizes on the ignorance of man to enforce his will upon him.

Here is wisdom for those who desire it: Satan is the driving force behind every form of worship that is demanded by force. Initially, it may be demanded by a subtle, harmless method, but in the long run, a covenant is introduced, and a death sentence is placed on defaulters. God does not operate like that. Such a method is of the devil.

> *Covenant is introduced, and death sentence is placed on defaulters. God does not operate like that, but such method is of the devil.*

THE ORIGIN OF SPIRIT HUSBAND AND WIVES

Let us consider who is a spirit husband or wife before tracing the origin.

A spirit husband or wife is a spiritual personality who demands a romantic relationship from human beings, willing to make that relationship permanent.

Spirit husbands and wives demand love, care, romance, sex, and intimacy from their human spouses or suitors. Why do they want a human personality? It is because they are bodiless spirits seeking a human to express their desire, lust, and ultimate action or reaction. Their main objective is to lead human beings to the side of their principal, the devil.

The origin of spirit husbands or wives can be traced back to Satan when, as Lucifer, he fell off from the side of God after his rebellion against God and whatever God stands for. He was cast out of the presence of God with his angels and those who rebelled with him. And a place called hell and a pit is already prepared for them. *"Yet you shall be brought down to hell, to the side of the pit" (Isaiah 14:15). Revelation 12:9* also speaks of this.

The origin of spirit husbands or wives is traceable to rebellious satanic spiritual personalities seeking strange flesh, having given themselves over to fornication *(Jude 1:6-7)*. According to the scriptures, they are the angels that kept not their first estate but left their own habitation. They are rebellious toward God and all that God stands for.

> *Sex is not an exercise to be performed in the dream; it is limited to the physical, and only with those joined together in marriage.*

Let this be clear, any spiritual personality that demands conjugal romantic relationship and sex, be it an angel or spiritual being, is definitely not of God, for the scripture says,

"In the resurrection they neither marry nor are given in marriage but are as the angels of God in heaven" (Matthew 22:30).

Angels of God in heaven do not demand marriage. Neither are they given out in marriage. Human beings too, at resurrection, shall be as angels of God. Here is another wisdom: sex is not an exercise to be performed in the dream; it is limited to the physical, and only with those joined together in marriage.

Spirit husbands and spirit wives are satanic spiritual personalities desirous of satanic wishes and options for mankind. And these satanic wishes are hinged on what the scripture says in the book of *John 10:10*.

"The thief comes not but for to steal and to kill and to destroy." Who is the thief? Satan.

> *Spirit husbands and wives can be very wicked towards their physical rivals. Sometimes they go to the extent of killing their rivals.*

ACTIVITIES OF SPIRIT HUSBANDS AND WIVES

In the earlier part of this book, I told a story of a woman who was completely ignorant of the existence of these spiritual beings.

On a particular public holiday, the husband left the bed very early in the morning for his study to carry out a specific official assignment. The man was in the study almost all day. Around 8:30 a.m., these personalities moved in to the bed with the woman. Naturally, the woman felt the presence of a man, mistaking him for her husband. And the woman was thoroughly and sexually dealt with by the personality. After the "hot" experience, the whole bed was messed up with semen and the personality left. Around 9:30 a.m., the woman regained her consciousness. Her husband was not there with her. She was confused, and she made a serious mistake: She went to her husband who was in his study and asked him what time he left the bedroom.

And the man said he had been in his study as early as 5:00 a.m. Still confused, she told her unbelieving husband what happened. She even led him to the bedroom to see the messed up bed and the rest. The husband reacted sharply. That was the end of her marriage.

Those evil personalities had succeeded in throwing the woman out of her matrimonial home so that they could keep her for themselves all the time.

Spirit husbands and wives see the physical husbands and wives as rivals, and they hate them greatly since they are very jealous of their perceived spouses.

Spirit husbands and wives can be very wicked toward their physical rivals. Sometimes they go to the extent of killing their rivals.

> *All the words of endearment like dear, sweetie, and darling uttered by women are from lips. In fact, such endearments are only done in the presence of visitors. Immediately when the visitors are gone, the man is back into his personal prison cell.*

Many people have lost their husbands or wives to the activities of spirits husbands or wives. I know a woman who has lost about three husbands to death. She has become miserable. Some of these spirits even appear physically to her in the house.

There are some women who enjoy the relationship with the spirit husband more than their physical husband. The love, care, and loyalty that are to be for their physical husband is diverted toward their spiritual personality. The physical husband is treated like a slave in the marriage. The man experiences hell here on earth. The woman has a terrible hatred, contempt, and no regard for the physical husband. The man, the physical husband, is hated everywhere he goes. He enjoys no favor both in his office and everywhere. Sometimes, he is rendered poor and naked. And the wife is fat and plump; whereas, the physical husband would be ill fed, getting skinny and sickly all the time.

The man can lose all inhibition and not be able to think straight or positively. This is because he is operating under serious oppression of both his wife and her spirit husband.

> *Such women are so crafty, pretentious, subtle and desperately wicked. Only God can deliver such men from their hands. Sometimes, they can weep very sore to whip up sentiments in order to carry out their wicked agenda.*

Oppression makes the wise man mad (Ecclesiastes 7:7).

The man will remain under the yokes and bondage of his wife and her spirit husband. When you see a woman who does not have regard for her husband but treats her husband with disrespect, check it out; she may be under the influence of this strange personality the spirit husband. All the words of endearment, like dear, sweetie, and darling, uttered by such women are just from the lips. In fact, all such endearments are only done in the presence of visitors, that is, Open Display of Affection (ODA).

The Mystery of Sex

When the visitors are gone, the man is back in his personal prison cell. But as many that are reading this book in such a bondage, the mighty hand of God shall deliver you in Jesus name. Amen.

The spirit husband, sometimes, can come even physically into the house, and only the wife will see him, and they will have a chat. Whenever there is a third party, the spirit disappears. Such women are never broke. Any amount they want to spend is made available to them by their spirit husbands. So they have total love for their spirit husbands while they have total hatred for their physical husbands. Such women enjoy regular sexual relationship with their spirit husbands while they starve their physical husband with sex. In fact, they don't allow their physical husbands to touch them. When they allow their physical husbands to touch them, they drop sickness and disease, evil deposits, or an arrow into their lives through sex.

Such women are never broke. Any amount they want to spend is made available to them by their spirit husbands. So, they have total love for their spirit husbands while they have total hatred for their physical husbands.

When such men seem to be enjoying sex with their wives, it is not enjoyment; an arrow is being shot into their lives, which could lead to installment death.

Some women can be so wicked that they would with their spirit husband not to have physical children for their physical husband. This is sometimes to divert the attention of the man to another problem while the real problems remain intact.

The woman and her spirit husband continually laugh and scorn the ignorant physical husband. Such women are so crafty, pretentious, subtle, and desperately wicked. Only God can deliver such men from their hands. Sometimes, they can weep very sore to whip up sentiments in order to carry out their wicked plans. Don't be carried away with their weeping, sometimes for their childlessness. It could be a wicked lie after all. The devil and his agents are really bad, terrible, and wicked.

> Sometimes their spirit wives would go physically, as girlfriends, to their offices; and as spirit wives to their homes. All the love, emotion, and care would be diverted to women outside; whereas, the woman at home and her children are starving.

To be quite honest, many people who are in this serious bondage are Christians. They are children of the Most High God whom God has ordained for specific purposes.

There are many pastors who are in this bondage. The enemy has crept into their homes unaware, and they are currently in serious trouble.

The fatal and sad thing about this situation is that, if such men die in their state, it's because they have allowed their destiny to be manipulated by the enemy through their so-called wives.

God cursed Adam for hearkening to the voice of his wife, though God knew it was Satan that deceived Eve, Adam's wife.

The Mystery of Sex

"And to Adam he said, because you hast hearkened unto the voice of your wife. . . . Curses followed" (Genesis 3:17).

If you are reading this book and you know that you have no voice or say in your own home, in fact, sometimes you are afraid to confront your wife, the woman whose dowry you paid, you cannot even challenge her misbehavior probably because she's the one feeding the entire family, know for sure that the power behind that woman will drag all of you to hell fire if you fail to take a divine step. God ordained you as a man to rule over your woman.

Husbands who have spirit wives operate almost like a woman with a spirit husband. The wives of such men never enjoy their marriage. In fact, such men hate their wives with perfect hatred. No matter how beautiful the woman at home may be, they still have extramarital affairs outside. They are always pushed out of their marital bed by their spirit wives.

> *All the wearing of trousers, exposure of sensuous parts of the body, seductive dresses, walking almost naked on the streets are the manipulations of these powers.*

These are men who always desire to "taste" almost all women who are attractive to them. They are never sexually contented. Sometimes their spirit wives go physically as girlfriends to their offices and as spirit wives to their home. All the men's love, emotion, and care is diverted to women outside, whereas the woman at home and her children are starving. They could care less about the consequences of their actions.

Let us consider some scriptural insights in to the activities of these evil personalities called spirit husbands and wives.

"And it came to pass, when men began to multiply on the face of the earth, and daughters were born to them. That the sons of God saw the daughters of men that they were fair and they took them wives of all which they chose" (Genesis 6:1-2).

These sons of God decided to go in to the daughters of men contrary to the Lord's commandments. The products of that relationship brought forth defilement on the daughters of men.

Why are there powers willing to bring defilement upon women, the daughters of men?

As soon as man fell into sin through the disobedience of Eve, God spoke to the serpent, *"And I will put enmity between you and the woman, and between your seed and her seed; it shall bruise your head and you shall bruise his heel"* (Genesis 3:15).

> *Spirit husbands pollute the lives of their victims. They plant evil deposits into their lives. All the fibroid development in the wombs, false pregnancies, and barrenness are deposits of spirit husbands.*

These powers, which are agents of Satan, knew that it is the seed of the woman that shall destroy serpent—that is Satan, their master. They knew Jesus Christ would come as a seed of the woman. They decided to pollute every available woman so that the coming of the Holy One through the woman would be prevented.

The Mystery of Sex

This is still happening now. When a woman is scheduled to bring forth the prophet of God according to God's plan, these powers will push the woman into sin in order to give them foothold in the life of the woman.

Immediately after a door is opened for them into the woman's life, they move in to bring about serious defilement upon the woman.

All the wearing of trousers, exposure of sensuous parts of the body, seductive dresses, and walking almost naked on the streets are the manipulations of these powers. Once a lady is involved in any of these things, the coming of the spirit husband becomes a walk over.

Through counseling, we have had a lot of experiences. A lady was married for many years without an issue. This sister knew she had a spirit husband that regularly had sex with her, after which she was losing her pregnancies. This had been her situation for so many years. Then she came to us for prayers. After series of hot prayers, she noticed that the spirit husband stopped coming to her.

Before the prayers, she was counseled never to wear trousers again, which she promptly obeyed. One day, as she was in a vigil praying, she observed there were mosquitoes at the venue. She then excused herself to put on a pair of trousers under her long gown to prevent mosquito bites.

> *A Brother also complained that somebody sucked his manhood in the dream, and ever since the incident, he could not perform in bed with his wife; but he could do well with the spirit wife.*

After the vigil, she went to rest somewhere. That night, the spirit husband that had disappeared for some times resurfaced, and he thoroughly romanced and sexually molested her.

The lady confessed that the sexual act that night was hotter than any of her previous experiences. She was astonished that it happened after prayers, and at the place where the vigil was held. Why? It's because she put on a pair of trousers, giving the spirit husband a foothold and a door to come in to her again.

On that very day, the sister burnt all the trousers she had and vowed never to wear trousers again.

> The surface of the earth everywhere is filled with evil spirits and the powers of darkness.

It is important to say this: all sisters who wear trousers will definitely have a spirit husband. They may not be conscious of it at the beginning, until a strong hold is erected by the evil power in their lives. This is real and true, no matter your personal opinion.

I have said earlier that spirit husbands pollute the lives of their victims. They plant evil deposits into their lives. All the fibroid development in the wombs, false pregnancies, barrenness, etc., are deposits of spirit husbands.

There are some sisters who are sexually insatiable. They can never be sexually contented. If it's possible they want to have sex every day. It's all as a result of the deposits of spirit husbands.

Sometimes sicknesses are planted in the victims' lives by this power. Kisses from spirit husbands could result in cough or tuberculosis, while touching or sucking of the breast could lead to breast cancer.

A sister complained that somebody sucked her breast in the dream, and since that experience, she had been having terrible pains on her right breast. Arrow of cancer must have been shot at that breast through the sucking by the evil spiritual personality.

A brother also complained that somebody sucked his manhood in the dream, and ever since the incident, he could not perform in bed again with his wife; but with his spirit wife, he could do well. Meanwhile, this brother was diagnosed as having a low sperm count. These are activities of spirit husbands and wives.

How to Acquire Spirit Husbands or Wives

A lot of people acquire spirit husbands or wives through various means and methods. However, we need to be conscious of the environment in which we find ourselves. We also need to be conscious of the manifold presence of God and darkness around us or within us. God is light, and darkness is absence of light. What does this mean? Darkness is not a positive creation. It's just the absence of light or where God of light does not manifest, though God is present everywhere, including hell. Heaven is His throne, and the earth is His footstool.

> *In the spiritual realm, these evil spirits are everywhere. Sometimes, they move with winds or with other elemental forces.*

Let us consider some scriptural insights into the war that took place in heaven.

"And there was war in heaven, Michael and his angels fought against the dragon and the dragon fought and his angels. And prevailed not neither was their place found any more in heaven.

And the great dragon was cast out, that devil and Satan, which deceiveth the whole world, he was cast into the earth, and his angels were cast out into the earth, and his angels were cast out with him. Therefore rejoice ye heavens and ye that dwell in them Woe to the inhabitants of the Earth and of the sea for the devil is come down unto you having a great wrath, because he knoweth that he hath but a short time" *(Revelation 12:7-12).*

A careful look at this scripture would bring out some important facts:

> *Spirit husbands or wives could have been acquired through ancestral lines or inheritance.*

1. The place of the devil or dragon and his angels can no longer be found in heaven.
2. Those who inhabit or dwell in heaven will live in joy and peace continually due to absence of the devil and his angels.
3. The earth now has an evil visitation and a tale of woe that is upon those who dwell or inhabit the earth because the devil and his angels are cast out into the earth.

In consideration of these facts, it is clear that the devil has taken possession of the earth with his angels. No

The Mystery of Sex

wonder the Bible refers to him as the prince of this world.

This means practically everywhere on the surface of the earth is filled with evil spirits and powers of darkness.

This situation confirms what happen in *Genesis 1:2*: "And Earth was without form and void; and darkness was upon the face of the deep. And the spirit of God moved upon the face of the waters."

The situation in *Genesis 1:2* is still relevant and true. The darkness we are talking about is not physical but spiritual. It is the absence of light or absence of God. It is where God does not manifest. Darkness is the presence of the evil angels or spirit beings that are cast out with Satan into the earth. These are unseen evil personalities that inhabit every spectrum of the deep. Even in Science, we talk about the magnetic field that covers the entire surface. These are invisible but surely existent. In the spiritual realm, these evil spirits are everywhere. Sometimes they move with winds or with other elemental forces. This is why somebody would say a cold breeze blew at him and he was paralyzed. This confirms their presence.

> *The spirits attached to the waist bands could transform to spiritual husbands or wives of the innocent victims.*

"And the spirit of God moved upon the face of the waters" (Genesis 1:2).

A careful student of the Bible would discover that the waters refer to peoples—that is, human personalities.

In *Revelation 17:15*, the Bible says, "The waters which you saw, where the whore sits are peoples, and multitudes and nations and tongues."

And the Spirit of God that moves upon the face of the waters is the light of God that is seeking to penetrate into the heart of men, to lighten up their darkness.

And Jesus said, "Behold I stand at the door and knock; If any man hear my voice and open the door I will come into him and will sup with him and he with me" *(Revelation 3:20).*

> **And demons are attached to the waist bands, causing sexual lust which are active and reactionary.**

Unfortunately, the great whore is already seated upon them all. She has taken possession of them all. This is why human beings have familiar spirits. And these familiar spirits could have existed through blood line from a generation to generations. It can only take the presence of God; that is, Jesus Christ, the light of the world, to chase away the power that is resident in many lives.

In short, spirit husbands or wives could have been acquired through ancestral lines or inheritance. In our environment, evil spirits are everywhere. Only the manifest power of God can hinder them from carrying out their evil assignments.

From the analysis made above, it is clear that spirit husbands and wives can be acquired through parental inheritance.

Evil Dedication

Africa is a place of idol worshipping. Idol worshipping is prevalent in Africa from generation to generation. The evil is being passed down to children and children's children even till now. Ancestral fathers have dedicated generations of their children to idols.

Our group went to a village and we preached to a woman who claimed to be a worshipper of Sango. She referred to herself as "Mama Sango." This woman told us that her parents worshipped Sango, and she was born into that worship. She claimed that all her children were given to her by her god, Sango, and she was ready to die worshipping Sango.

The evil testimony of this woman confirms the fact that she must have been dedicated to the idol even from the womb, for when a life is dedicated to an idol, that idol has a stronghold on such a life.

There are lots of evil personalities that claim to be husbands of all female children in a particular family, while some evil female personalities claim to be wives of all male children in the family.

The waist band that is used as a protective charm for children at tender ages is a means of evil dedication. The spirits attached to the waist bands could transform to spiritual husbands or wives of the innocent children.

The beads used by ladies to provoke sexual desires for them from their male counterparts are all satanic means of leading the ladies to their spiritual husbands.

To be quite honest, ladies that mostly wear waist beads are either agents of a marine kingdom or are about to get initiated into the marine. Demons are attached to the waists beads to activate sexual lust that is active and reactionary.

All bondages of the hips could be very infectious to male and female. They result in destruction.

Multiple Spiritual Husbands or Wives

It is very possible for an individual to acquire multiple spiritual spouses. In fact, it makes the bondage stronger and difficult to break. A lot of people go to places and unconsciously pick up one or two demons. This is why it's tragic for children of God to be attending night parties, night clubs, brothels, et cetera.

Your presence in some places could increase the number of spiritual personalities that would keep harassing you. There are places where there is heavy traffic of evil spiritual personalities. Places like shrines, occultic meeting places, palaces, hotels, brothels, night clubs, cross roads, beach, cinema houses, et cetera. There is no way one can appear in such places and not acquire one or two demons. And when a sister dresses half naked to such places, surely, multiple evil personalities will bombard her life. So places you go can increase the yoke or bondage of spiritual spouses.

How to Escape

The escape route is the way of life that can only be found in Christ Jesus. "Jesus said I am the way, the truth and life, no one comes to the father but by me" *(John 14:6)*.

And the Bible says, "In him was life and the life was the light of men, And the light shines in darkness, and the darkness comprehends it not" *(John 1:4-5)*.

The Mystery of Sex

To escape is to allow the light of God in your life to dispel every form of darkness in you. When there is fullness of Christ in a life, no dark spirit can come near that life. Unfortunately, the truth of the matter is that our flesh is always alive to accommodate these evil powers. This is why the Bible says we must mortify the deeds of the flesh. Our flesh must die. It profits nothing. "The flesh does no good, it is the spirit that quickens, the flesh profits nothing" *(John 6:63)*.

Mr. Flesh must die. But Mr. Flesh is very stubborn and rebellious. It has to be mortified daily. We must lay our body on the altar and be sacrificed. This is what Jesus did on the cross. He killed the flesh on the cross so that the spirit could be resurrected back to life.

We, Christians, should be prepared to go to that place of the skull, a place of slaughter, the cross, to kill Mr. Flesh and all its attendant problems and power.

Mr. Flesh accommodates these powers in order to deal with our inner man—our spiritual personality.

We must not pamper the flesh. We must mortify it and its deeds. Then we should wage war and battle violently against these powers. They are very wicked. We too must not have mercy on them. This is because they want to destroy us.

Sexual intercourse is an exercise that brings about deep spiritual implications on our lives. Casual sex could lead to serious problems, death, and/or eternal doom.

CHAPTER NINE

THE ACTIVITIES OF SOUL (HEART) KIDNAPPERS

The activity of the heart kidnapper may sound very strange to many people. In fact, quite a lot of good men are victims of this power, yet they are ignorant of their activities. A lot of lives and destinies have been ruined and cast down through the operation of this power.

In Africa, this power operates from locality to locality, and the spiritual environment is favorably conducive to their operations. Both men and women fall victim to the evil effect of this satanic power.

If a woman was a child when her marriage was contracted and she cannot get out of it when she is grown up, though she does not like it, she is a victim of the evil power.

If a brother had to marry a sister as a result of an unwanted or unplanned pregnancy, or if he unconsciously married a sister but later finds himself in a marriage he does not like and cannot get out of it, he could be a victim of men kidnappers.

The greatest and most effective weapon of male kidnappers is sexual intercourse. It operates and works like a bait and a hook. Once the targeted prey is hooked, or yoked together with a power greater than him or her, such a prey can only be delivered by God Almighty.

The issue of sexual relationship must be very carefully examined before one is involved. The Bible says, *"When a man received the Lord's commandment; he shall incline his ear to wisdom and apply his heart to understanding"* (Proverbs 2:2).

> *When a man receives the Lord's commandment, he shall incline his ear to wisdom and apply his heart to understanding.*

An understanding heart is fundamental to survival in this wicked world.

In the book of *Revelation 18:11-13*, the Bible talks about the merchants of the earth who merchandise gold, silver, precious stones, pearls, fine linen, purple, silk, scarlet, thyine wood, all manners of vessel of most precious wood, brass, iron, marble, cinnamon, odors and ointments, frankincense and wine, oil, fine flour, wheat, beast, sheep, horses, chariots, slaves, and *"SOULS OF MEN."*

Is it not strange that after many years of abolition of slave trade, there exist traders whose stock are slaves and souls of men?

Sometimes ago, something strange happened in a village, in the south western part of Nigeria. A man had a very large farm running to acres of land on which he planted various crops. The strange thing about this farm is that nobody was ever seen working on it either with tractors or simple agricultural tools such as hoes, cutlass, et cetera. But the farm was always seen to have been worked upon. You'd never know the time the job was done.

One day the son of the owner of the strange farm saw his father washing his face with the water in a pot buried inside the ground. The young man secretly did as his father without knowing the implication. Then he saw many people known to him had died in the village. They were working hard on the strange farm.

> *The souls of those men have been captured with satanic power and have been sentenced to hard labour on a strange farm.*

The souls of those men were captured with satanic power and sentenced to hard labor on the strange farm. These men must have been killed through various means, which may have included sexual contact. The major weapon of soul traders is sexual intercourse.

It is important to note this: The greatest strategist among the fallen angels that fell with Satan is the power called "The woman of Babylon." The great whore that sits upon many waters. *And the waters being sat upon are people, nations, and tongues (Revelations 17:15).*

This power operates in all places of the earth, in fact, in every land where human personalities exist. This

The Mystery of Sex

power, according to the scriptures, is sometimes called marine power or the great dragon that lies in the midst of its rivers *(Ezekiel 29:3)*. In some places, the power is called the Queen of the Coast. In Yoruba land, it is called Olokun Spirit or Queen of the Niger. The power has all her human agents, both male and female, everywhere. Sometimes it is called "mammy water spirit." The power has an image of a woman with a fish tail. Her girls are mostly very beautiful and her males are very handsome and rich. They ride in flashy cars and live in great affluence. They are highly connected to men at the corridors of power. Sometimes they are rulers of nations. The Bible says *"The kings of the earth [presidents, governors, et cetera] have committed fornication with her" (Revelations 17:2)*. When there is a sexual relationship with one of their agents, one automatically becomes one

> *Children and great grandchildren can be sold off even before they are born.*

of them. They capture souls of men and women and hand them over to Satan. They are drinkers of blood and eaters of flesh.

Jesus is described as the Bridegroom of the church. At the last day, the triumphant Church shall be married to the Lamb of God at the great feast called the marriage supper of the Lamb *(Revelation 19:8-9)*. Satan too, through deceits and subtlety, desires worship from men so that their souls will be united with him in hell. This is why many agents of Satan trade out the souls of men forcefully. The Bible talks about power that sells nations and families: *the well-favored harlots, the mistress of witchcrafts that sells nations through whoredom and families through her witchcrafts (Nahum 3:4).*

Only one witch in a family can sell ten generations of the family to Satan. Children, grandchildren, and great-grandchildren can be sold off even before they are born. Sometimes, souls are exchanged for money, power, fame, et cetera.

Some politicians go into occultism to seek political power. In the process, they sell off their children even to the tenth generation, all for fame and political power. And these transactions are usually done through sex.

The bottom line is that souls could be sold out to Satan through sexual contact, and it is imperative that we understand this and jealously guide our lives from satanic activities.

> *The bottom line is that souls could be sold out to Satan through sexual contact, and it is imperative that we understand this and jealously guide our lives from satanic activities.*

Men's Hearts Kidnappers into Marriage

I said earlier that a lot of people enter into marital covenant ignorantly only to find out that they have been yoked together with a child of the devil. And when a child of God is yoked together in marriage with a child of the devil, he or she will experience marital hell here on earth. All the blessings of marriage automatically become curses and bondage for him or her.

The children of darkness are so merciless and brutal, especially toward those who are in the light. This is why the Bible warns: *"Be you not unequally yoked together with unbelievers for what fellowship has righteousness with unrighteousness and what communion has light with darkness? And what concord has Christ with Belial or what part has he that believes with infidel? And what agreement has the temple of God with idols?" (2 Corinthians 6:14-16).*

Many temples of God have been converted to idols through marriage. A scriptural example is King Solomon who loved many strange women. The Bible says, *"For it came to pass, when Solomon was old, that his wives turned away his heart after other gods and his heart was not perfect with the Lord his God, as was the heart of David his father" (1 Kings 11:4).*

> *To be quite honest, it's only God Almighty that can reveal the thoughts of the hearts. Your partner may be very pleasant, nice, supporting and seemingly loving, but deep inside his or her heart, the agenda might be to kidnap your soul for destruction and eternally marry you to Satan.*

Satan understands the potency of marriage in turning away the heart of people of God toward strange gods and idols. He, therefore, uses the agents of darkness in that direction to kidnap the hearts of men.

At this juncture, I will examine their weapons and style of operations.

THE HEART KIDNAPPERS

Are you in a relationship now that you think it's good enough to blossom into exchange of marital vows? You need to examine yourself very well, especially if you are not born again, and/or if the foundation of that relationship is sinful. You might have fallen victim to heart kidnappers. Examine yourself and that relationship very well. To be quite honest, it's only God Almighty who can reveal the thoughts of the hearts. Your partner may be very pleasant, nice, supporting, and seemingly loving, but deep inside his or her heart, the agenda might be to kidnap your soul for destruction and eternally marry you to Satan. This does happen to most people who are God-fearing and God-lovers.

> *If a sister sprinkles a love potion on a brother's food, as soon as the brother eats the food, he begins to fall in love with her... Immediately the evil love affair leads to a sexual relationship the sister's mission is accomplished.*

To examine yourself and your relationship properly, the very first thing to do is to get out of the relationship. Then ask for forgiveness of sin and purification of your body, soul, and spirit by the blood of Jesus, especially if you have had sex with your partner. It is after that you can examine and see clearly the original position or the true personality of your partner.

If you allow that sinful relationship to blossom into legal marriage, the bondage and the yoke become harder and stronger. A young, successful businessman was in a relationship with a tall and beautiful sister. Eventually, they got married. A few years after marriage, the brother's business collapsed. After serious prayers, the brother knew the cause of his problems could only be traced to the wife. He said his marriage with the sister was impromptu, and he could not remember at what point he decided to go into the marriage. He just found himself in it.

The heart of that brother might have been kidnapped. When he regained his consciousness, the evil had been done. The marriage had produced children, and God forbids divorce. The brother had to continue in the unpleasant marital relationship, hoping only for God's intervention.

The major weapon of men kidnappers is still a sexual relationship; however, there are other weapons that are employed to activate and manipulate their target into sexual relationship.

Food

The devil's agents can use love potions to hook their victims. If a sister sprinkles a love potion on a brother's food, as soon as the brother eats the food, he begins to fall in love with her. As a result, he establishes a romantic relationship with her. Immediately then the evil love affair will lead to a sexual relationship, and the sister's mission is accomplished. He will never again see anything bad in the life of that sister, even when his friends and relations make genuine complaints about her. He would stick to his passion for the woman, as he has been forcefully united with her in the spirit realm. At this level, the sister would be fully in charge of the brother's life. The brother would be deaf to all advice of his friends, even parents.

A sister narrated how life fish could be used as a love potion to capture a man. The kind of fish normally used for this purpose is life mud fish. When a sister conjures and unites a brother's spirit and hers on the fish, the moment the brother eats the fish, he will fall completely in love with the sister.

> *Do you know that some ladies do wash their private parts and use the water to prepare food for men just to win their hearts.*

It is important to say this— no matter how many people eat the pepper soup, the targeted brother would be singled out for its direct impact since his name was used for the love potion.

Many lives have been captured through this method. A lot of people with very bright stars and destinies have been caged. Do you know that some ladies wash their private parts and use the water thereof to prepare food for men just to win their heart?

Other things that can be used to manipulate people into relationship are clothes, underwear, rings, and other personal effects. Sometimes gifts can be used. To be honest, it is only prayer that can neutralize all these satanic tools of manipulation.

That relationship you are in, has it not subjected you to a serious witchcraft manipulation? You need to examine that relationship through repentance and prayers.

The Mystery of Sex

When someone is operating under the devil's manipulation, he can never perceive any inherent danger.

Let us consider what happened to a great man of God in the book of Judges.

"And it came to pass afterward that he loved a woman in the valley of Sorek, whose name was Delilah". . . . And Delilah said to Samson tell me I pray you wherein your great strength lies and wherewith you, mightiest be bound to afflict you" (Judges 16:4,6).

This woman called Delilah did not hide anything from Samson. When you consider the question she asked him: "What is the source of your great strength and power so that I can destroy that source for me to afflict you?" And Samson did not perceive the danger around him, yet he divulged the source of his great strength to his enemy, Delilah. And what happened to Samson? He died with his enemies.

> *Men kidnappers are very merciless and brutal. They have no respect for their husbands, neither do they love them. They see their husbands as slaves and treat them as such. But in courtship before marriage they can pretend to be the best person on earth.*

Samson must have been operating under serious manipulation. Only God knows what Samson ate on the table of Delilah before the sexual relationship with her.

If a sexual union is established with a person who has the devil's mandate to bring people into hell, it will be very easy for the person to manipulate the prey into achieving his/her own selfish motives. This is why many housewives rule over their husbands. Many of them are anointed to work for Satan.

A woman came for deliverance, and the Holy Spirit revealed to the man of God in charge that the woman was not ready for deliverance. She did not want to part with her satanic power. And the power was the cause of her family's problems. The woman confessed that if she relinquished the power, she would be done for, as she was employing the power to manipulate her husband, and she was always getting whatsoever she desired from him. She therefore did not want to live without the power, though it was sucking her blood.

> A kitchen is generally regarded as the wife's office in the house. Therefore, once a sister possesses it spiritually, she has taken possession of the bedroom and even the entire life of a brother.

Men kidnappers are very merciless and brutal. They have no respect for their husbands; neither do they love them. They see their husbands as slaves and treat them as such. But in courtship, they can pretend to be the best person on earth. They often offer their would-be spouses a lot of gifts to lure them into serious relationship. If they discover their fiancés to be lovers of God, they give them a close monitoring,

The Mystery of Sex

leaving no stone unturned till they accomplish their evil mission.

Here is wisdom for bachelors: Do you allow your fiancée to cook for you? Do you allow her to enter into your kitchen? If you have prayed and God has confirmed your choice to you, no problem, but if she has succeeded in luring you into her life, you may be on a journey toward affliction and death.

The devil's agents are cunning. They have many spiritual ways of working themselves into their target's life. For instance, a sister could bring a stool usually used in the kitchen into a brother's house. She would have done some rituals on it. Once the sister sits on the stool right in the brother's kitchen, she has spiritually taken over the marital life of that brother, since her seat is already in the brother's kitchen.

A kitchen is generally regarded as the wife's office in the house. Therefore, once a sister possesses it spiritually, she has taken possession of the bedroom and even the entire life of a brother. If the possession is done through satanic means, immediately after the marriage is contracted, Satan moves into the home and empowers the woman for destructive agenda.

Brothers must be very careful. When a brother sleeps with a satanically anointed sister, it becomes very easy for the sister to capture his heart.

If any man is already inside the web of men kidnappers, he should pray to God to destroy their network and cage. A brother who truly repents and prays can be released from such a bondage. If he realizes this before it's too late, he will not suffer much.

CHAPTER TEN

SEXUAL ATTRACTION, SEDUCTION, AND PERVERSION

"There shall be no whore of the daughters of Israel nor a sodomite of the sons of Israel" Deuteronomy 23:17

VARIOUS FORMS OF SEXUAL PERVERSION: THE ROOTS OF MARITAL PROBLEMS

If you are called to the service in God's vineyard and your destiny is programmed along God's plan and purpose in his kingdom, let it be clear to you that Satan has a definite agenda for your life, because he will not fold his arms, watching you destroy his kingdom. This is to say that you are a target of the devil, for you are dangerous to his kingdom and purpose.

Jesus, the Son of God, who was born into the world to redeem mankind from the power of darkness and to restore them to God, had terrible confrontations against his purpose, even in His infancy. Immediately after he was born, some wise men were able to locate his star. As the news of the appearance of his star reached Herod, he and all that were with him in Jerusalem were troubled. Herod therefore made efforts to destroy Jesus.

The Mystery of Sex

Every minister of God, who must have escaped such an attack in infancy, still has sufficient onslaught awaiting him as he grows and proceeds in his calling and ministerial duties.

When you are called, God will prepare you adequately for the assignment before you. He will nevertheless expect you to be consecrated to Him. He will not want you to go outside the sanctuary nor desecrate His sanctuary.

The sanctuary we are talking about is your body, which belongs to God. It must be kept Holy for God to dwell therein. *There is a crown of anointing oil of God upon the head of those that are called (Leviticus 20:10).*

The crown of anointing oil of God is the spiritual empowerment of those who are called. This is the target that Satan seeks to pollute and destroy. It must be guided very jealously. Samson failed to jealously guard his own. A woman, daughter of philistine, shaved off his locks, and the crown of God's oil on him was removed. Samson then became powerless, and it ended in tragedy.

> The crown of anointing oil of God is the spiritual empowerment of those that are called. This is the target that Satan seeks to pollute and destroy. It must be guided very jealously.

The crown of God's oil on the head of every minister is Satan's target. An effective power that can remove it is the power of sexual attraction to the opposite sex. There is a serious battle going on between the crown of oil on your head and your sexual attraction.

WHAT IS SEXUAL ATTRACTION?

It is that thing that is present in every man and woman that makes members of the opposite sex desire to have sex with him or her.

The flesh is so formidable in every man and woman that, until it is mutilated, no man or woman can go along with God. The killing or mutilation of the flesh should be a daily affair for a minister to move forward in God's business. This is why the flesh is against the spirit and the spirit against the flesh. One is contrary to the other so that you cannot do the things that you should do *(Galatians 5:17)*.

> *The flesh is so formidable in every man and woman that until it is mutilated, no man or woman can go along with God.*

The desire of the flesh, which is the Adamic nature of man, does not respect your level of anointing. No matter how heavily a man or woman is anointed, the fleshy nature in the anointed is still formidable and capable of ruling over his or her willpower, unless the flesh is dead. This is why a man or woman, when involved in dry fasting for days, should not engage in arguments or fight any one. No matter the insult, he/she should not respond to any verbal attacks. Why?

It is because, during the period of fasting, the flesh that is expected to respond is subdued through fasting.

The Mystery of Sex

This is why fasting and prayer is fundamental to the spiritual development of anyone who decides to work with God.

The spirit man in the life of every individual is the location and the indwelling place of God. This is why the Bible says, *"the spirit of man is the candle of the Lord" (Proverbs 20:27)*.

It is the spirit of man that the spirit of God will locate for habitation. And the spirit of God that dwells in man bears witness of those who are children of God.

"The spirit itself bears witness with our spirit, that we are the children of God" (Romans 8:16).

God wants to live in us. He also wants us to live in Him. But Satan, our enemy, wants to hide under our flesh to paralyze the potential. God has deposited in us. The flesh, therefore, always wants to push us into sin, knowing that when we live in sin, the nature of God in our spirit man will be paralyzed and rendered powerless for demons to take over and rule over our entire life. However, with fasting and prayer, the flesh is paralyzed, and the Spirit of God rules over our life.

> *Your fiancée is still a strange woman until she's married to you. Your relationship with her could be a snare from the kingdom of darkness to arrest your destiny.*

Satan and his agents hate the children of God. They always seek to push them to sin in order to paralyze the nature of God in them. Their quickest and most effective weapon of attack against men of God is sexual sin.

Sexual sin can instantly bring a man of God to the level of a piece of bread. And once a life is reduced to a piece of bread, it will be wasted easily.

The Bible warns all expressly not to lust after the beauty of a strange woman.

Who is a strange woman? Any woman, lady, or girl who is not your proclaimed wife, such is a strange woman.

Bachelors know this: Your fiancée is still a strange woman until she's married to you. Your relationship with her could be a snare from the kingdom of darkness to arrest your destiny. So beware. Once you engage in a sexual relationship outside the will of God, you may not be alive again to tell the story about your life or that relationship.

The Bible says, *"For the commandment is a lamp; and the law is light, and reproofs of instruction, are the way of life."*

> *Your life in a wicked generation or in the midst of enemies is like a journey in the wilderness or dark places of the earth.*

Your life in a wicked generation or in the midst of enemies is like a journey in the wilderness or dark places of the earth. Your strategy against stumbling is your obedience to the Lord's commandments and law. The commandment of the Lord is a lamp to your feet, and the law is the light to your paths. And the reproof of instructions is the road to life, or way of life. Any contrary opinion could only lead you to destruction and death.

The Mystery of Sex

This commandment of the Lord is aimed at keeping you away from evil.

'To keep you from the evil woman, from the flattery of the tongue of a strange woman.

"Lust not after her beauty is your heart, neither let her take you with her eyelids. [Some eyelids can be very powerful].

"For by means of a whorish woman a man is brought to a piece of bread and the adulteress will hunt for the precious life" (Proverbs 6:24-26).

This passage is saying that life is very precious and can therefore be hunted and turned to a piece of bread.

The Lord's solution to problems of mankind is still patterned along the same line from generations to generations, even till now. That pattern is sending down a leader to lead mankind away from destructions and death.

Abraham was called out to bring forth generations of the Lord's heritage. Moses was sent to lead God's people out of the Egyptian bondage. Jesus Christ was sent to lead mankind out of sin and death to salvation.

Sending down a leader is God's method still.

> *The commandment of the Lord is a lamp to your feet, and the law is the light to your paths. And the reproof of instructions is the road to life, or way of life.*

The Satan's method is to attack the leader. He knows that once the leader is attacked the flock will scatter. Every one called into the ministry is assigned to lead a particular group of people. This is why God's ministers must be very careful the way they live their lives.

God sent down Samson to deliver his people from the oppression of the Philistines. It was an Angel of God that announced his birth and his purpose. Unfortunately, Samson allowed a woman, daughter of God's enemies, the Philistines, to destroy his life and his purpose. Samson therefore died with his enemies.

In the Church of God today there are many daughters of Philistines who are assigned by Satan to bring down the anointed men of God.

The Bible says, *"Let not your heart decline to her ways, go not astray in her paths for she has cast down many wounded; yes, many strong men have been slain by her. Her house is the way to hell, going down to the chambers of death" (Proverbs 7:25-27).*

> *Ministers! Beware. There is a vulture of death hunting for your precious life.*

A man of God had been in the service of the Lord for many years. He was very faithful and was heavily anointed by God. But he never knew a vulture of death was assigned against his life and ministry.

A lady member of his congregation was monitoring him, pretending to be zealous for God, both in church activities and social duties.

This man of God was transferred to another place. Three months after, this same sister surfaced in the city where the man of God was posted. She lied that she too was there on transfer by her company.

The Mystery of Sex

After seventeen years of close monitoring, she succeeded in getting the man of God. It happened that his wife travelled and the "nice" sister who was helpful to him both in cooking and house hold ministration, eventually carried her "help" to the bedroom. After the unholy exercise, the lady smiled and declared, "After seventeen years of close monitoring, our mission is now accomplished." And she disappeared, leaving the man of God in the bedroom stone dead. How are the mighty fallen.

Ministers! Beware. There is a vulture of death hunting for your precious life. *Let not your heart decline to her ways, lust not after her beauty, neither let her take you with her eyelids.*

Vultures can be very patient in achieving their objectives. Imagine an operation that took seventeen years to accomplish.

A fellow minister once asked, "How could a minister who knows the truth fall prey so easily?"

I told him, "Every man or woman has his/her unique desire for the opposite sex."

This desire is that thing that makes a woman attractive to a man and a man to a woman. For example, some men like women who are fair in complexion and slim, whereas, some prefer those who are plump.

The desires for these traits defer from one individual to another. Therefore, it is important for an individual to marry a spouse who satisfies his/her desires.

> *Vultures can be very patient in achieving their objectives. Imagine an operation that took seventeen years to accomplish.*

God knows us more than we know ourselves. If God decides somebody's choice in marriage, the attraction and love between each other will remain ever green. Unfortunately, Satan has misled quite a lot of people to wrong partners, but then, with prayer, such marriages could still be healed by God, if the people submit to Him wholly in time.

In effect, every man or woman has a peculiar compulsive sexual attraction toward the opposite sex. It is inside every individual.

Let us consider the scriptural insight into this salient truth. Man inside woman and woman inside man.

"So God created man in His own image. In the image of God created he him; MALE AND FEMALE created He them" (Genesis 1:27).

> *Some men like women who are fair in complexion and slim; whereas, some prefer those who are plump. The desires for these traits defer from one individual to another.*

According to this passage, man and woman had been created as an entity, even before God had to form the first man, Adam, out of the dust of the ground.

In the spiritual realm, man and woman had existed in each other. In chapter two of the same book of Genesis:

"God now formed man of the dust of the ground and breathed into his nostrils the breath of life" (Genesis 2:7).

"And the Lord God said, it is not good that the man should be alone, I will make him a helper" (Genesis 2:18).

The Mystery of Sex

"And the Lord caused a deep sleep to fall upon Adam and he slept, and took one of his ribs, and closed up the flesh instead there off. And the rib, which the Lord God had taken from man, made he a woman, and brought her to the man. . . . This is now bone of my bone and flesh of my flesh; she shall be called a woman, why? because she was taken out of man" (Genesis 2:21-23).

According to this passage, in every man, there is an existing woman who is latently created with him *(Genesis 1:27)*. And that woman who is bone of his bone and flesh of his flesh is somewhere. In the same way, there is a man meant for every woman.

For the purpose of our discourse, inside every man, there exists a woman. In fact, it is scientifically proven that the seed of a man determines the sex of a baby. That is to say, the man determines the sex of a baby. Man's seeds produce both X and Y chromosomes, meaning that inside every man there is a woman.

> *So, it can be said that inside everyman there is an "Eve" (woman), that provokes the desire to be attracted to the outside woman who conforms to the image of the one inside.*

So, it can be said that inside every man there is an "Eve" (woman) that provokes the desire to be attracted to the outside woman who conforms to the image of the one inside.

No wonder when a man touches a woman in the dark, he will know she is a woman. Satan knows this truth, and he uses it against everybody.

There are some women who can never be attractive to some men. So the men can't lust after such women. Satan is aware of this and matches only those who conform with each other's desires. This is why flesh must be crucified daily and be dead to any form of lustful desire.

Any woman sent to destroy a minister will usually be the kind he desires, so that he will unconsciously fall into sin. This kind of temptation does not exclude any one, no matter the level of your anointing.

> They have eaten satanic peppersoup and they are now obeying satanic command of the strange woman. Careless eating has led a lot people into serious bondage.

In fact, Jesus Christ was equally tempted at all fronts. *"For we have not an high priest which cannot be touched with the feeling of our infirmities, but was in all points tempted as we are; yet without sin" (Hebrews 4:15).*

How was Jesus Christ tempted by fleshly desires? Let's consider the scriptures.

And behold, a woman in the city which was a sinner, when she knew that Jesus sat at meat in the Pharisees' house, brought an alabaster box of ointment. And stood at his feet, behind him weeping, and began to wash his feet with tears, and did wipe them and kissed his feet and anointed them with the ointment. Luke 7:37-38.

Then took Mary a pound of ointment of spikenard very costly, and anointed the feet of Jesus and wiped his feet with her hair and the house was filled with the odor of the ointment. John. 12:3 A very beautiful woman came to anoint the feet of Jesus with very costly ointment. She wiped His feet with her long hairs, and kissed his feet. How many of God's ministers today can stand a woman wipe their feet with her hair and perfume? Some ministers while holding the hand of a woman to pray with them are already transfixed with lust. God's ministers must be dead to all those fleshy lusts and desires. Jesus was equally 'tempted in all points like as we are; yet without sin'. Hebrews 4:15. No one has any excuse to fall into temptations. The sexual attraction of individual minister, either a man or woman is the number one enemy of his anointing, calling and destiny. It must be dealt with without further delay, before it brings shame, reproach and even death upon the life and calling of the man of God.

THE POWER BEHIND SEXUAL PROMISCUITY

Any form of sexual sin brings God's judgment on the culprits. When a sexual sin is committed by God's ministers, or God's people, it instantly turns God against such people. And the wrath of God is waxed hot against them. This gives Satan power over such people of God. He then brings them to destructions.

Balak hired Balaam to curse the Israelites. God had to intervene, and Balaam was stopped from carrying out the destructive assignment. The Lord God then converted the curses into blessings over Israel. Balaam declared by the word which God Himself put in his mouth: How shall I curse, whom God has not cursed? Or how shall I defile whom the Lord has not defiled?

Rather than curse Israel, Balaam blessed Israel. Balak took Balaam to another high place, peradventure it could be possible for him to curse Israel. Seven altars were erected, and a bullock and a ram were offered as a sacrifice on every altar. Afterwards, Balak asked Balaam what the Lord has spoken. And Balaam answered him again with the words which God put in his mouth saying:

God is not a man, that he should lie; neither the son of man that he should repent; has he said and shall he not do it, or has he spoken, and shall he not make it good? Behold I have received commandment to bless, and he has blessed and I cannot reverse it. He has not beheld iniquity in Jacob, neither has he seen perverseness in Israel, the Lord his God is with him and the shout of a king is among them. (Numbers 23:19-21).

It was not possible for Balak and Balaam to bring curses upon God's people, Israel. And Balaam rose up and returned to his place. Balak also went his way. Numbers 24:25.

And later something strange happened. The people; I mean Israel, began to commit whoredom, a sexual sin, with the daughters of Moab. And Israel joined herself to Baalpeor and the anger of the Lord was kindled against Israel. And a plague entered in among them. In one day, twenty thousand died in the plagues.

"And those that died in the plague were twenty and four thousand! (Numbers. 25:9).

The Mystery of Sex

These are God's people, who could not be cursed before. But when they fell into sexual sin, the curse of God, anger of God, waxed hot against them, and they died.

How did this happen? A power provoked them into sexual sin, knowing that as soon as they fall into that sexual sin, their God would turn against them.

It was the same Balaam who could not bring the curse upon them that gave the evil counsel saying: let Israel commit sexual sin with the daughters of Moab which would turn their God against them. And immediately Israel fell into sexual sin, there was a serious plague among the congregation of the Lord.

"And Moses said to them, Have you saved all the women alive? Behold these (women) caused the children of Israel, through the counsel of Balaam, to commit trespass against the Lord in the matter of poor, and there was a plague among the congregation of the Lord." Moses had to command all the women of Moab that have known man by lying with him to be killed. (Numbers 31:15-17).

When your enemies have tried various options to attack you and did not succeed, the next available option left for them is to send a woman who would provoke you to sexual sin. And immediately you fall, they would fulfill their agenda.

On our streets today are many ladies and men empowered by Satan to destroy lives and destinies through sexual immorality. A lady had sex with an occultist. Shortly after the exercise, she went mad.

How would one explain this situation: A man was being ministered to in prayer. As prayers were going on, he pulled off his trousers. Behold, what represented his manhood was a serpent. Following a serious prayer session, the serpent left his life, and his manhood became normal. The question now is what has befallen the ladies he had previously slept with? Many of them must have been destroyed. When such sisters or brothers approach children of God that have no sufficient fire, they may not be able to resist their seductive invitation to immorality. This is because they have been empowered by Satan to cause destruction. At this juncture, it is better to analyze in details how these powers operate so that children of God would be able to recognize them.

POWER MAGNET FOR SEXUAL SEDUCTION

THE EYES

Job seemed to have a proper understanding of the danger inherent in using his eyes to behold women. He understood that it could lead him into serious troubles. He therefore made a covenant with his eyes never to think upon a maid. Job. 31:1

Many of the so called beautiful ladies in our environment today have very powerful eyelids. And they can fully use such eyelids to their satisfaction. Quite a lot of men have been captured by satanically empowered eyelids.

The Bible says *"Lust not after her beauty in your heart, neither let her take you with her eyelids." (Prov. 6:25).*

The Bible does not waste words: '...neither let her take you with her eyelids'. This means it is possible

The Mystery of Sex

to capture men with eyelids. To be frank, through the eyes, arrow of lust could be fired, and if the targeted prey does not have sufficient resistance, the arrow will prosper. Before you say Jesus is Lord, you'll see a full grown man, going after a small girl as an ox goes to the slaughter. Many ministers have been captured with eyelids while they were ministering. This is because they didn't have sufficient resistance. Why the arrows get into people's lives is because there is an enemy within. The enemy is the lust of the heart and the lust of the eyes. Let consider what Jesus told His disciples.

"But I say to you, that whosoever looks upon a woman to lust after her has committed adultery with her already in his heart. (Matt. 5:28).

When a man lusts after a woman in his heart, he's already guilty. He has sinned against God by committing adultery of the heart. This gives the devil a chance to impose his will upon the man.

Through the eye, a life could be polluted; and when a spiritual life is polluted, it gives entrance to all sorts of demonic personalities. This gives the power of darkness unlimited opportunities to oppress, torment, repress, possess and even kill. This is a very serious matter. We must be very careful about the usage of our eyes. We should not allow our eyes to control our life.

Job said, *'if my step has turned out of the way and my heart walked after my eyes'... (Job 31:7).*

From this scripture, it is possible for the heart to walk after the eyes. And when a heart walks after the eyes, the owner could be led astray, and end up in destruction. Our hearts must therefore be guided jealously. The Bible says we should keep our heart with all diligence, for out of it are the issue of life. Proverbs 4:23.

The Lord GOD wants us to submit our hearts to him totally. The devil too wants our heart. Once the heart of a man is captured by the devil, the battle of that life is already lost to the devil. How can you now allow your eyes to control your heart?

Immediately the heart is polluted through what you behold with the eyes, you have been defiled.

The eyes are very important and therefore must be kept holy with all diligence. Do not allow your eyes to pollute or defile your heart.

"Let your eyes look right on, and let your eyes lids look straight before you. Ponder the paths of your feet, and let all your ways be established, turn not to the right hand nor to the left, remove your foot from evil." (Proverbs 23:24-27).

This Scripture gives us the guide to the survival strategy in a perverse and wicked generation.

A lot of people will divert their journey while beholding strange women. Their hearts will turn after their eyes. And the diversion of paths, could earn them sudden death or destruction.

We are told to set our eyes to look right on, and that our eyelids look straight before us.

The Lord GOD knows our frame and our limitations as sinful man. Therefore, through His words, He tries to guide us in all truths. Satan, the enemy of man, also understands the frame of man. He knows how to lay snare to catch men. This is why quite a number of strange women are released from the kingdom of darkness to confuse men with their modes of dressing. They put on strange apparel to seduce men into sexual immorality.

Our eyes should not behold vanity; neither should they behold strange women. We must therefore guide our heart and eyes with all diligence in order to prevent every form of pollution. This is very important for all GOD's ministers.

THE MOUTH

The mouth is another way through which the devil has cut down many people. A lot of people have entered into serious bondage through the mouth gate. Many have left their homes for the bosom of the strange woman. Strange women have captured them, and they no longer find their wives' food delicious, but that of the strange woman.

The situation becomes so serious that some men, immediately after they collect their salary, go straight to the strange woman and drop everything. Afterward, they start regretting their actions. They cannot understand why they subjected their family to untold hardship and poverty.

They have eaten satanic pepper soup, and they are now obeying

> *As a minister of GOD, I have heard about different situations where a woman washed her genitals into a bowl and used the water to prepare meals for men to win their hearts.*

satanic commands of the strange woman. Such men can only be delivered by GOD through Jesus Christ, His Son.

Careless eating has led many men into serious bondage and trouble. Let us consider some scriptures on this.

Jesus saw a man who was born blind from his birth. And his disciples asked who sinned, the man or his parents?

"And Jesus answered, 'Neither the man or his parent sinned, but that the word of God should be made manifest in him.' And when he had spoken, Jesus spat on the ground and made clay of the spittle and anointed the eyes of the blind man with the clay and said to him 'Go, wash in the pool of Siloam,' and he went his way therefore and washed and came seeing" (John 9:3-7).

Jesus' spittle, his saliva, was used to make clay that he used to anoint the eyes of the blind man. And the blind man received his sight. This means that saliva can carry some supernatural power.

Do you know that human saliva can carry satanic power, and, depending on the wish of the user, satanically empowered saliva can perform some supernatural feat? Yes, it can. A woman wanted to serve a brother food one day but luckily, the brother

> *It is very sad, that some house maids have taken over the bedroom of their mistress or madam. The master now prefers the food made by the dirty looking house maid to that made by the madam.*

was somewhere, looking at her from afar, unknown to her. The woman spat in the plate deliberately. Not that she sneezed; she spat in the plate. Afterward, she dished steaming hot white rice on the spittle. She then served the meal with assorted pieces of meat, chicken, et cetera, to the brother. Though the brother was hungry that day, he cleverly declined eating the rice. GOD in His mercy allowed him to see the secret of the meal he was served. The question now is what was the mission of that woman? Many people have had such meals, and now cannot understand the mystery behind their problems.

Let us analyze what could be the mystery behind that woman and her spittle.

In the first place, that woman's saliva represented her personality, as it came from her. If that brother had eaten the rice that day, he would have swallowed a human spiritual personality, which could have opened his life to spiritual attacks from the woman.

Secondly, that woman's spittle, being representative of her, could make it easy for the woman to seduce the brother.

As a minister of GOD, I have heard about different situations where a woman washed her genitals into a bowl and used the water to prepare meals for men to win their heart.

A lot of men have had fresh fish pepper soup prepared with such water. How can one explain a situation where a man, whose wife is not only beautiful but also dear and obedient, suddenly prefers the food prepared by a street vendor to meals his wife prepares? The truth of the matter is that the man could have ingested a love potion. This is real. It is still happening in our society today.

God's ministers are not exempted from this if they are careless with what goes into their mouths. Immediately after a man eats the food prepared with love potion, he can be subjected to sexual immoralities very easily.

It is very sad that some housemaids have taken over the bedroom of their mistress or madam. The master now prefers the food made by the dirty-looking housemaid to that made by the madam.

We must be very careful with what goes into our mouth. A minister of GOD was given a gift of wine by a member of his church. He decided to keep the wine. Surprisingly, a strange tree grew inside the bottle of wine, the following day. That was the wine given to the man of GOD.

I really feel sorry for some sisters who get married to husbands who are not born again. Those who are married to husbands who drink, smoke, and commit immorality with strange women need to pray very hard. This is because not only the life of the man but also that of the wife and the children are seriously exposed to danger.

> Sisters, whose husbands still stay where bottles roll, need serious prayers for the deliverance of their homes from the power of the grave.

Let us consider what the Bible says, "Who has woe? Who has sorrow? Who has contentions? Who has babbling? Who has wound without cause? Who has redness of eyes? They that tarry long at the wine, they that go to seek mixed wine" (*Proverbs 23:29-30*).

This scripture is saying that any man who goes to beer parlor is full of woes. In fact, there is no hope for such a person except he repents. But if not, his life shall be characterized by wounds, redness of the eyes, and all sorts of contentions and woes.

"Look not you upon the wine, when it is red, when it gives its colour in the cup, when it moves itself aright. At last, it bites like a serpent, and stings like an adder. Their eyes shall behold a strange woman and your heart shall utter perverse things. Yes, you shall be as he that lies down in the midst of the sea, or as he that lies upon the top a mast. They have stricken me shall you say, and I was not sick. They have beaten me and I felt it not: when shall I awake? I will seek it yet again" (Proverbs 23:31-35).

When a man reflects soberly on this scripture, he discovers that a beer or wine addict has no hope at all. He's a walking corpse ready to be buried at any time.

> Many adverts feature ladies in underwear, and the jingle used in such adverts are more often characterised by lustful melodies which provokes sexual urge.

The scripture says you should not look at the wine when it gives its color inside the cup or a glass, when it moves itself aright. The Bible says, "It bites like a serpent and stings like an adder." It makes you tipsy or intoxicated, then your eyes shall behold strange woman, a whore or harlot, and your heart will start meditating on immorality and you will start to speak perverse words.

An average drunk will open up his mouth and expose his valued secret to the enemy. His heart will run after a whore who is described as a deep ditch.

> *Good communication can minister grace to the hearers and, conversely, corrupt communication can minister corruption to the hearers.*

"For a whore is a deep ditch and strange woman a narrow pit" (Proverbs 23:27).

Many people have from the beer parlor entered into their grave and have been bound by the power of the grave. Beloved, most of the women who serve in beer parlors are empowered by the power of the grave. Their bottom that you enjoy touching is a way to hell, going down to the chambers of death *(Proverbs 7:27)*.

They are deliberately employed to catch men. Inside this women is the spirit of graveyard. The Bible says a whore is a deep ditch and a strange woman a narrow pit *(Proverbs 23:27)*. Sisters, whose husbands still stay where bottles roll, need serious prayers to deliver their homes from the power of the grave.

Look at another scripture. *"The mouth of a strange woman is a deep pit, he that is abhorred of the Lord shall fall there in"* (Proverbs 22:14).

May the Lord deliver many husbands that are in bondage before they fall into the pit, in Jesus name.

Ear

The ear is another gateway to spiritual pollution that could provoke evil sexual seduction. The Bible talks about corrupt communication. Corrupt communication could gender into sinful desire. And when it is done, it will minister corrupt practices that can defile the hearer. Evil communication can also corrupt good manners *(1 Corinthians 15:33)*.

What you hear can sometimes bring defilement to your life. It can provoke sinful desires. We must be careful about what we hear with our ears.

> *Jesus said, 'The word which I speak to you are spirits and are life' John 6:63. Conversely, the word of Satan are spirits and are death.*

The television has done so much havoc to moral standard in our society. What people see and hear on the electronic and new media (internet) provokes sinful desires in the life of teenagers. For instance, most advertisements on the radio and television and lately postings of porn/nude pictures on internet have contributed greatly to the sexual decadence in our society. Many adverts feature ladies in underwear, and the jingles used in such adverts are often characterized by lustful melodies that provoke sexual urges. These are satanic strategies designed to lead many astray and to push many into sin. We should be aware of this truth and be careful about what we see and hear on the electronic media. The Bible says, "Let no corrupt communication proceed out of your mouth but that which is good to the use of edifying that it may minister grace unto the hearers" *(Ephesians 4:29).*

This scripture says good communication can minister grace to the hearers and, conversely, corrupt communication can minister corruption to the hearers.

There are many slang words that have emanated from the worldly music. Such slang spreads like wild harmattan fire. The question is what is the source of those words? Who inspired the musicians that composed them?

> *Children that are used to reading the Bible will be filled with the word of GOD. They will be heavenly bound. And those that read the worldly literature will be filled with the lust of the world and then Satan will prepare them to perish with the world.*

Such slangs are from demonic spirits from the bottom of hell. And when a child of God speaks such demonic slang, he is booking a space for himself in hell fire, registering his name in the book of death. The devil knows that with the mouth, you shall be justified or be condemned, depending on the choice you make.

What we hear goes a long way in bringing defilement into our spirit.

LITERATURE

Another means of spiritual pollution that provokes sexual sin is satanic literature. Satan inspires some writers to produce these literatures to cause sexual sin among teenagers and youths.

The Mystery of Sex

There are quite a number of immoral magazines with pornographic pictures on the newsstands. This literature displays nude men and women in various sexual positions. Also there are romantic novels. Though they do not have pictures; they paint pictures of sexual acts with words that are obscene enough to arouse a sexual urge.

> *That man starring at your exposed boobs may have already polluted your life by throwing arrows of cancer into those breasts.*

As this literature is read, the spiritual personalities behind the immoral actions they contain are transferred to the readers. This is why many people find themselves doing what they read in their dreams. In fact, a lot of people acquire spiritual wives and husbands through these literatures.

Sexual stories instantly provoke a lot of people to sexual immorality. To be quite honest, it is possible to acquire HIV, even through the reading of pornographic literature, without necessarily having sexual contact with anybody. This is because the spiritual personality can enter into the spirit of whoever reads these immoral magazines and literature. We have heard of cases of virgins who are HIV positive. The truth being exposed in this book may sound strange, but it is real.

These are snares Satan have set to catch the souls of men. The Bible says, "My people are destroyed for lack of knowledge." To be ignorant of these things and be involved is to prepare for calamities, woe, sorrow, and death.

People have read some books and ended in psychiatric hospitals. And teenage girls have been provoked to prostitution through reading of immoral literature.

> *Arrows can be fired with the eye. Why do you wear garments that expose the sexual parts of your body? It is an invitation to self-destruction.*

Jesus said, "The word which I speak to you are spirits and are life" *(John 6:63)*. Conversely, the word of Satan are spirits and are death. All the immoral words, suggestive of sexual lust, carry satanic power. And they lead teenagers and youths to immorality. Parents must be aware of these facts and therefore scrutinize the kinds of literature being read by their children. This is very important since children who are used to reading the Bible will be filled with the word of GOD. And they will be heavenly bound. Whereas those who read the worldly literature will be filled with the lust of the world then Satan will prepare them to perish with the world. In fact, some children who get addicted to these things could go very far with the world; to bring them back to life could be extremely tasking and difficult.

It is better they are never exposed to this evil in their tender age. Parents must not be careless on this matter. The world we are in is full of corruption, pollution, and wickedness. Serious Christian parents must ensure that their children escape this trap of the enemy.

Immoral literature is a magnet for sexual immorality. And we must understand this truth and be careful about things we read and watch.

STRANGE PERSONALITIES AMIDST HUMAN BEINGS

I would like to say very clearly that human personalities on the surface of the earth have different levels of power and anointing. Man can move in the power of God or in the power of the devil, depending on the choice they make. Man can appear physically and disappear into thin air.

> *When a man or woman has sex with evil spiritual personalities, golden arrows will be released into his or her life.*

There are angels of God that move physically in the midst of men. The Bible says, "Those angels are greater in power and might" *(1 Peter 2:12).*

In a church with a large congregation, where there are manifestations of God's Power, angels come in disguise of worshippers.

In fact, angels do bring answers to people's prayers by coming to sit by their sides physically. When the man of God says all eyes close, and he begins to pray, that is the time the blessings are released to the congregation's spiritual beings.

Angels are spirit beings, but they can appear physically. They are ministering spirits that are sent forth to minister to them that are heir of salvation *(Hebrews 1:14).*

Angels are sexless; they can appear as male or female. This is why brokenness, humility, meekness is preached to the brethren. These are the fruits of the spirits that determine your sonship in the Lord. It is this nature of meekness, which is of God, that confirms your status as a child of God. Jesus told his disciples to love one another so that people will know that they are his disciples in deed. If you love your fellow with all your heart, you will not curse him or her for any reason. I would like to say that when a man of God asks you to pray for the fellow by your side, it is to ensure the release of blessings sent through the angels upon the owners.

Angels stick to rules of the game. Sometimes, when angels get to the owner of the blessing and the fellow does not behave in conformity with the rules, the angels can decide not to release the blessing and go back with it or give it to another person. Beloved, the brother or sister you have abused could be the angel God sent to give you answers to your prayers.

It is not every man or woman you see by your side who is a human personality. We must therefore be very careful. This truth may sound strange; it is real.

Also Satan sends his dark angels to human personalities. They too move about to cause confusion in the midst of the human race.

Some of the ladies who go about in sensuous dresses, exposing their bodies, invite serious troubles into their lives. Satan hates women seriously. Therefore, when a woman puts on a strange apparel in defiance of God's commandments, she facilitates the job of the dark angels.

That man staring at your exposed boobs may have already polluted your life by throwing arrows of cancer into those breasts. Arrows can be fired with the eye. Why do you wear garments that expose the sensual part of your body? It is a way to self-destruction.

A lot of ladies acquire spirit husbands every day through the sensual garments they wear. Many sisters

The Mystery of Sex

have multiple spirit husbands who appear and disappear at will. The existence of these spiritual personalities is no news especially these last days.

In the book of Acts of the Apostles, Apostle Phillip ministered to the Ethiopia Eunuch by baptizing him in the water. "Immediately, the spirit of the Lord caught away Phillip that the Eunuch saw him no more" *(Acts 8:39)*. And Phillip was found in Azotus. Passing through, he preached in all cities till he came to Caesarea.

Phillip went without travelling from Samaria to Azotus. He disappeared in Samaria and appeared in Azotus. This means Holy Spirit can catch away men physically. This is the power of God.

For every good thing God has for His people, Satan has a corrupted replica for his followers. People have bought apples while travelling and disappeared only to appear before an altar in a shrine in the forest for sacrifice.

These satanic strange personalities are with us daily. A woman died in a town in Ekiti State and was found selling food at Ojuelegba in Lagos. As the fellow who knew her in her previous life in Ekiti called her name, she disappeared. Everyone around trembled.

A woman went to defecate in the bush, and as she was there, she saw a big python transforming to a human being. She was transfixed, seeing a beautiful girl emerged from the snake. A few minutes after, she left the bush and saw a foolish man driving a Mercedes Benz car carry the snake girl in his car.

We have heard about a case of a man whose manhood is a snake. Serpents have run out of private parts of many sisters after hot prayers. Two serpents ran out of a sister sometime; one was killed, and the other ran away.

So all these strange personalities are different from unseen demons. Those demons are bodiless spirits. In fact, Satan can allow about six thousand demons to follow every individual on the surface of the earth *(Mark. 5:9)*. These strange personalities are often married to normal human beings.

The point I am making now is, do you know that fellow you are dating? When a man or woman has sex with evil spiritual personalities, golden arrows will be released into his/her life. In fact, sometimes prayers may not help such people because they are already joined together with the evil personality. Besides, their life could have entered destruction. Death could be instant or gradual. Many people have died but still work about. Such people are walking corpses.

Sex is not an exercise in which man should indulge like dogs. It is sometimes an open grave; once a life enters, he may not come back to life again.

Sexual perversion of any type is rebellion against God and His commandments. It is encouraged by the devil and his agents, with the aim of turning children of God to God's enemies. When a man or a woman enters into the web of Satan through any form of sexual perversion, he is instantly abhorred by God.

There are spiritual personalities behind every form of sexual perversion. These personalities are the powers that push men and women into all forms of perversion. There have been testimonies of people who were

The Mystery of Sex

found in shameful sexual acts. They confessed, "I don't know what came upon me and got me into this evil and shameful deed."

A University lecturer woke up one day beside his beautiful wife around 1:00 a.m. and went to his boys' quarters where he saw his house girl sleeping naked. Immediately, a strong force pulled the highly respected professor toward the girl. But as he was having sex with the girl, his wife woke up and traced him to the boys' quarters where she astonishingly caught the two right in the sexual act.

The force that pulled that man toward the dirty-looking house girl is the power behind shameful sexual acts. It is imperative for men and women to have proper understanding of such forces, their tricks, and how they can be dealt with to escape the satanic program of shame and destruction in this wicked world.

ADULTERY

Adultery occurs when a married man or woman engages in sexual intercourse outside marriage.

A woman committed adultery sometime ago, and she entered into a serious trouble. I'm not sure whether she has gotten out of the trouble as at the time of writing the book.

The woman, with her husband, was in her cousin's party when she saw her former boyfriend. Immediately, she became restless. She

> *The force that pulled that man towards the dirty looking house girl is the power behind shameful sexual acts and actions.*

then held a bottle of water and left her husband secretly to meet her former boyfriend in a dark corner.

Meanwhile, when her husband did not see her, he thought she was on assignment, since it was her relation's party. He did not know that his "dearest" wife was already having sex with another man, her former boyfriend. But as faith would have it, after the woman and her "lover boy" had satisfied their sexual urge in a dark shop, away from the party, she took a bottle of water to clean up her private part. Unfortunately, it was a bottle other than the one she took there. It contained acid, not water; for the shop was a battery charger's workshop. She poured the acid on her private part, thinking it was water. And she screamed, for her genitals were promptly eaten up by the acid.

Sex is exclusively meant for married couples. A death sentence awaits all adulterers and adulteresses" *(Leviticus 20:10)*. Also, wound and dishonor await them *(Proverbs 6:33)*.

> People whose parents are accomplished fornicators and adulterers are very likely to continue in their parents' unholy deeds.

FORNICATION

Fornication is the sexual relationship between unmarried couples. Sexual relationship between a married man and an unmarried lady is adultery to the married man and fornication to the unmarried lady involved. The bottom line is that they are involved in sexual pollution and defilement. And judgment of death and destruction awaits all fornicators and adulterers *(Leviticus 20:10, I Corinthians 6:18-19)*.

The Mystery of Sex

Homosexuality

This is sex between two male partners. It is a sexual relationship between two men. This evil is common these days. In fact, men are now being joined together in unholy wedlock. Homosexuals are even seeking rights of recognition. The Bible says it is abomination and death sentence that awaits all homosexuals" *(Leviticus 18:22).*

Lesbianism

This is a direct opposite of homosexuality. It is sexual relationship between two female partners. The Bible says it is an abomination *(Leviticus 20:22).*

Incest

This is "sexual relationship between male and female who are each other's next of kin." For example, it is a sexual relationship between father and daughter or between son and mother or between sister and brother of the same parents or between cousins.

> *And judgment of death and destruction awaits all fornicators and adulterers.*

The Bible says, "None of you shall approach to any that is near of kin to him to uncover their nakedness I am the Lord" *(Leviticus 18:6-16).*

Masturbation

This form of perversion is very common because it appears harmless to many people. It is giving self-sexual satisfaction through touching or stroking one's sexual organs. When a man or woman does that, a spirit-being takes over the actions. And that fulfillment derived must have been energized by the spiritual personality called spirit husband or wife. When someone is masturbating, he is sending a love advances to demons, inviting them for sexual affairs. Masturbation, precisely, is having sex with demons. It is a serious abomination *(Jude 1:6-8)*.

> *Masturbation precisely, is having sex with demons, and it is a serious abomination.*

MASOCHISM

This one is very strange. It is when a woman enjoys sex only after she is seriously beaten. Do you know some ladies do not enjoy sex except they are thoroughly beaten? After a serious beating, the women enjoy sex more. In fact, this happens among married men and women.

RAPE

This is when a man enters into sexual relationship with a woman by force, against the wish of the woman. Usually the man could have gained entry into the woman's vagina by the reason of his greater strength, which makes it possible to overpower the woman. Sometimes, rape is carried out at gunpoint. The woman, being fearful, just gives in without resistance.

Armed robbers had violated quite a lot of women, even young girls at the full glare of their parents. Many husbands had watched their wives helplessly being violated by evil men at gun point. Bad boys, in schools, have violated a lot of girls through rape.

The judgment of God against this evil is "death sentence" *(Deuteronomy 22:25)*.

SEXUAL RELATIONSHIP WITH FATHER'S WIFE OR CONCUBINE

Having sexual relationship with one's father's wife or concubine attracts a curse, for the word of God says, "A man shall not take his father's wife, nor discover his father's skirt *(Deuteronomy 22:30)*. The man named Reuben, who did it in the Bible received a curse from his father—for it was written of him: "You shall not excel because you went up to your father's bed, then defiled you it; he went up to my couch" *(Genesis 49:4)*.

And Reuben never prospered. He never excelled. Many are in serious trouble today because they slept with their father's youngest wife or concubine, and an anti-excellence curse is pursuing them day and night.

ORAL SEX

This is when a woman uses her mouth in lieu of her reproductive organ to give a man sexual pleasure. It is a serious sexual crime before the Lord God and the entire creation.

BESTIALITY

This is when a woman or man has sex with animals. A lot of ladies do have sex with dogs while some men have sex with fowls. The Bible says having sex with animals or a beast is confusion. Death sentence awaits all that practice this evil *(Leviticus 18:23)*.

> *The powers of the dog are ever stubborn, unrelenting in pursuing the anointed.*

PEDERASTY

This is when a grown-up man is fond of sleeping with young boys.

GIGOLOS AND GIGOLETTES

Gigolo is sexual relations between a young man who is paid to love an older woman called a sugar mummy. Gigolette is a sexual relationship between a young girl and an old man, who is called sugar daddy.

These sexual arrangements destroy so many lives and destinies. Many of these old men and women could be occultic, who usually use the lives of their sexual partners to renew their own lives or for money making rituals. Most of the times, they use money as a bait to hook their younger sexual partners. This sexual game between young and old couple could be destructive, especially to the younger partners.

> *Do you know that some ladies do not enjoy sex except they are thoroughly beaten? After a serious beating, the women enjoy sex more.*

PROMISCUITY

This is indiscriminate sexual desires and urges that can never be satisfactory. Some people can have sex throughout the night, non-stop. In fact, some people can never do without having sex in a day. To them, sex is a daily affair. This is why, when their spouse is not available, they are ready for just anything available to satisfy their sexual urge. There is a demon behind this act. Anyone living this kind of life needs serious deliverance.

Prostitution

This is having sex with someone for certain benefit. "Money for hand, back for ground." There are people who take to prostitution as a profession. They are called sex workers. There are others who seek for one benefit or the other, such as a promotion at work places or success in examinations. When someone is ready for sex to get benefits, that fellow practices prostitution, no matter how crude or decent the fellow may be.

Lasciviousness

This is when someone is involved in any trade, practice, venture, or business that promotes sexual immorality. It is also when your action, dressing, or speech triggers sexual lust that ultimately leads to sexual immorality. Examples are: pornography, indecent body exposure through evil fashion, and writing stories and publishing same in other to promote sexual immorality. All who are involved in this act can never be innocent before their Creator. The wrath of God awaits them, unless they repent.

> *A lot of things happen during sleep. We then need to understand the enormity of satanic onslaught upon men generally.*

Whether you are a journalist or you sell or market garments that promote immorality, you are as guilty as the actual offenders. The Bible says you shall not partake in another man's sins.

IDOLATRY

The combination of the various forms of sexual perversion is called Idolatry *(Colossians 3:5)*. And idolatry is a serious crime against God who is a jealous God.

TELEPATHY WITH THE OPPOSITE SEX

This is a form of unvoiced communications between two opposite sex lusting after each other through the eyes or unholy touch. The Bible says, "Lust not after her beauty in thine heart, neither let her take thee with her eyelids" *(Proverbs 6:25)*. This means men can be caught with eyelids. Telepathing with opposite sex could gender into whoredom thus bringing about perversion. Lust in the heart brings condemnation to the culprits before the Lord *(Matthew 5:28)*. Telepathy is an abomination before the Lord.

> *This sexual game between young and old couples could be destructive, especially to the younger partners.*

WHOREDOM AND CAUSES OF WHOREDOM

Various kinds of sexual perversion can be summarized in one word: whoredom. It is a Biblical name given to sexual immoralities or sexual relationship outside God's plans and ordinances. In the book of Ezekiel the Bible talks about two women, the daughters of one mother who committed whoredom in Egypt *(Ezekiel 23)*.

In the book of Revelation, the Bible talks about a great whore who's awaiting the judgment of God. This

The Mystery of Sex

is the power behind all illicit sexual distortions and perversion by men and women. This power, the Bible says, has made men, kings of the earth, and in fact all the inhabitants of the earth, to drink the wine of her fornication *(Revelation 17:1-2)*. It is the spiritual personality pushing men and women, great and small, young and old into a great sin: whoredom. It is therefore important to understand what whoredom is and its causes.

> *Whether you are a journalist, or you sell or market garments that promote immorality, you are guilty as the actual offenders.*

WHAT IS WHOREDOM?

Whoredom, as I said earlier, is sexual immorality in its entirety. Any form of sex outside God's rules and ordinances is called whoredom.

THE POWER BEHIND WHOREDOM

Whoredom is effectively masterminded by a spirit, which the Bible refers to as a "great whore." It is the same spirit the Bible refers to as the Babylonian woman called Jezebel who sometimes pretends to be a prophetess of God. She uses the fake prophetic anointing to teach and seduce God's servants into fornication and eating things sacrificed to idols *(Revelation 2:20)*.

PURPOSE OF THIS GREAT WHORE

The ultimate purpose of this power is to make God's people His enemies by bringing great defilement upon them, to pollute, kill, and destroy human beings despite God's plan for them.

The agenda is to steal virtues of God's people, destroy God's prophets, and bring them to ridicule and shame to prepare them for everlasting destruction in hell fire.

Major Causes of Whoredom

> *Telepathy with the opposite sex could lead to whoredom thus, causing perversion.*

Lust of the eyes: In the earlier part of this book I have mentioned the dangers that lustful eyes could bring upon a life. The fallen nature of man results in three principal spiritual problems: lust of the eyes, lust of the flesh, and the pride of life *(I John 2:15)*.

The eyes of God's people must be brought under thorough subjection. If not properly controlled, it could lead one to whoredom. I have said earlier that the evil spirit encourages whoredom. And most of these evils being done by these evil spiritual personalities are done in the dream. The Bible says, "While men slept, his enemy came and sowed tares among the wheat and went his way" *(Matthew 13:25)*.

A lot of things happen during sleep. We then need to understand the enormity of satanic onslaught upon men generally. Many acquire this strange anointing during sleep.

A dog bite in the dream: When someone dreams of dog pursuing him or her in the dream, the spirit of whoredom is at work.

Whorish food and drinks in the dream: For example, when a man or woman finds himself/herself being fed in a romantic manner in the dream, the spirit of whoredom is at work.

SPELL OR JINX: A spell or jinx could be put on someone. When a man always gets out of his bed by 1:00 a.m. and starts looking for a she-goat for sex, he is, without doubt, under a spell. Only God can deliver him.

SEDUCTION: Seduction can lead to whoredom. Some ladies through dressing know how to seduce men into immorality with their dressing.

> *Any form of sexual distortion outside God's rules and ordinances for sex is called whoredom.*

PORNOGRAPHY: Nude women and naked men featured in a magazine can lead to whoredom.
Also, the situations below can lead to whoredom:

- Dreaming and seeing oneself in the midst of many members of the opposite sex in the dream
- Being a man in the midst of various naked women in the dream or a woman in the midst of naked men in the dream.
- Seeing the city of members of the opposite sex in the dream
- Seeing the nakedness of members of the opposite sex physically
- Seeing the opposite sex naked in the dream
- Reading romance literature, books such as mills and boom
- Watching indecent films and movies
- Having Sex in a dream

- Infatuation and or unholy intimacy between members of the opposite sex
- Telepathy—when a lady looks at a man lustfully and they communicate with each other.

Indecent thoughts
—When whorish demons follow someone either physically or in the dream
—Sexual soul tie
—Whorish arrows
—Indecent wares and dresses

WHORISH GIFTS: Examples are romantic greeting cards, flowers, indecent text messages/e-mail et cetera, unholy touch, or handshakes with the opposite sex.

GENETIC FORNICATION AND ADULTERY: People whose parents are fornicators and adulterers are very likely to continue in their parents' unholy deeds.

BLEACHING AND DEMONIC COSMETICS: These are perfumes that have sensuous appeal. They trigger off fornication and adultery. Demonic hairstyle, hairdo or haircut (particularly hairstyles among ladies that are common to marine agents), and ladies' use of hair attachments can lead to whoredom.

BEAUTY AND HANDSOMENESS

When a woman is so beautiful that she gets attraction anywhere she goes, or a man is very

> *The power of the dog can stir up rebellion against the anointed, creating a kind of open confrontation. There are lots of Absaloms fighting their spiritual fathers in the house of God today.*

handsome to the extent that ladies always smile at him, such a woman or man is not far from whoredom. Marriage in the dream can lead to whoredom. Lastly, when a demonic dog is following someone spiritually, it is an invitation to whoredom.

CONSEQUENCES OF WHOREDOMS

- Defilement—*Romans 12:1*
- Sin against God—*Genesis 39:9*
- Sin against self—*Proverbs 6:25-35*
- Sexual soul-tie and life would be remotely controlled.
- Blood covenant
- Sexual bondage
- Change of destiny
- Breaking of home, or even breaking of courtship or relationship
- Spiritual dryness and backsliding
- Sicknesses, infirmity, and premature death

All of the above are offspring of whoredom to any child of God

CONSEQUENCES OF WHOREDOM FOR GOD'S MINISTERS

- Loss of Spiritual power and anointing
- Loss of respect of men
- Loss of ministry
- Loss of income

It is important that you apply the blood of Jesus to purge every strange blood and evil deposit resident in your life.

- Loss of relationship with family members
- Loss of relationship with Holy Spirit
- Loss of the kingdom of God
- Open shame before God and man

These are the problems that follow God's ministers who go into whoredom.

THE POWER OF THE DOG AND THE ANOINTED

There is a power recorded in the scripture as "the power of the dog." These powers, called the power of the dogs, are never friendly, but wicked, especially to the anointed ones. The psalmist said, *"For dogs have compassed me the assembly of the wicked have inclosed me, they pierced my hands and my feet" (Psalm 22: 16).*

David, the king of Israel, was highly anointed to carry out a great feat for God. He was referred to as the man after God's heart. Jesus, the Son of God, was called "the Son of David." The destiny of David was informed by God's program for mankind. David had a sevenfold anointing with seven spirits of God.

David was a king with kingly anointing, anointed to rule in dominion. He also had a priestly anointing. He had the anointing of a great warrior. His hands could fight and his fingers could wage war. He was a man of war. He also had the anointing for

> *Such can easily be controlled or manipulated under heavy yoke by the soul mate because an obsessive affection arising from soul tie is already formed.*

praise and worship. In addition, he had the anointing for prayer, the anointing for understanding, the wisdom, and the fear of God. The seven spirits of God were fully in him, and they manifested in his life and times. He ruled in dominion over his enemies and his generation. No wonder he performed a great feat for the Lord in his days. However, his exploits were not without opposition. He faced a fierce battle with the power of dogs. David said in the book of Psalms, *"For dogs have compassed me the assembly of the wicked have enclosed me, they pierced my hand, and my feet" (Psalm 22:16).*

The power of the dog attacked David's hands, the symbol of his labor. His feet were also under the attacks of this power. He had to cry to the Lord God, "Deliver my soul from the sword and my darling from the power of the dog" *(Psalm 22:20).* It is this same power that led David into adultery with Bathsheba, the daughter of Eliam, wife of Uriah the Hittite. And the grave sin of adultery that David committed brought upon him, his home, and his kingdom a curse from God: *"Now therefore, the sword shall never depart from your house, because you have despised me, and have taken the wife of Uriah the Hittite to be your wife" (2 Samuel 12:10).*

The consequences of that curse are still with Jerusalem today.

The power of the dog can turn God against His anointed. His own children. That is why He put a difference between the Egyptians and the Israelites. He decreed that *"a dog should not move his tongue against any children of Israel" (Exodus 11:7).*

When God's children are living a life of separation and sanctification, no dog can move its tongue against them. However, it is worthy of note that the power of the dog is always seeking to attack and destroy God's children and to pollute the anointing of God upon the anointed.

The powers of the dog are ever stubborn and unrelenting in pursuing the anointed. This is why many see dogs pursuing them in their dreams. All cases of dog bites in the dreams are indication that dogs are at work, and very close. God's ministers must wage war against the power of the dog, and should never relent in the warfare against the power. They must also watch very carefully in ministration, counseling, daily life, and activities.

The operation of this power against the anointed is not controvertible; it is proven to be a hard fact and a reality. The power of the dog can stir up rebellion against the anointed, creating a kind of open confrontation. It was this power that operated in the life of Absalom, David's son, who sought to take over the throne of his father. There are lots of Absaloms fighting their spiritual fathers in the house of God today.

This power sometimes operates silently or subtly just to pitch the heart of others against God's anointed; that is, the anointed leaders. They silently build up a formidable army within a church or an organization. They silently carve out an empire for themselves with a selfish motive. Absalom did it against his own father.

The Mystery of Sex

Anointed leaders must not sleep the sleep of death because this power could go very far before they realize the effect of its operations. Leaders must remain spiritually alert and alive to scatter every enclosure of the power of the dog before it is too late. These powers have their agents among men and women. Their agents may seem to be zealous for God's work. Anointed leaders must not be carried away by their zeal. This is why it is very important to depend solely on Holy Spirit before a leader takes any decision in the house of God.

David cried out "Dogs have compassed me." Every man, greatly anointed by God, will surely face attack from this power. Ministers of God must realize this hard fact and mount up a formidable defense against its satanic operations.

WHAT TO DO: ESCAPE ROUTE

If anyone is found in the trap of Satan through any of the discussed forms of whoredom, the first thing to do is to realize the sinful nature of the acts and repent immediately. The Bible says, *"Agree with your adversary quickly, while you are in the way with him" (Matt 5:25).* If something tells you or condemns you about your guilt in any of these abominable practices the best thing to do is to agree and repent quickly. Then plead for mercy and pardon, and you shall be forgiven.

The next thing to do is to run to Jesus for salvation of your soul. And when you are convinced of your salvation, go into deliverance prayer so as to eject every evil spirit resident in your life. It is imperative that you apply the Blood of Jesus to purge yourself of every strange blood and evil deposit resident in your life. You also need to ask the Holy Spirit to gather together all the fragmented parts of your life and destiny. Until they are put together again, you can't be sure of your breakthrough. You will then get going again.

Prayer Session

Preamble

When a man or woman is enslaved in any form of sexual perversions, such a person is already in the bondage of Satan and under the yoke of blood covenant. The person can be easily controlled or placed under heavy yoke by the soul mate. This is because an obsessive affection arising from soul-tie is already formed. He or she cannot think straight independently without the unholy influence of the other partner. This is a serious witchcraft bondage that takes only the power of God Almighty to break.

If you are in this unholy union or bondage, as you pray these prayers with genuinely repentant heart, the power of God will deliver you, in Jesus name.

Scriptures/Confession

Leviticus 18:1-30, Romans 1:18-32, Gal. 6:17: "From henceforth let no man trouble me for I bear in my body the marks of the Lord Jesus" *(Romans 8:2, I Corinthians 6:17; Romans 6:14)*. But he that is joined to the Lord is one spirit.

1. Serious praise/worship
2. Confession of sins and prayers for forgiveness: Mention the names of your sexual partners one by one. You should make a list of names you can remember. Mention them and renounce the unholy union with them one after the other.
3. I release myself from all unprofitable friendships, in Jesus name.
4. By the blood of Jesus I renounce my association and friendship with (mention the name of the person), and I break his/her power over my life, in the name of Jesus.
5. I come against every dark power that has manipulated me *(Mention your name)*, in the name of Jesus.
6. I command all evil remote controllers to lose their hold upon my life and affections, in the name of Jesus.
7. By the blood of Jesus, I remove myself from any strange authority ever exercised over me.
8. I come against every desire and expectation of the enemy to engage me in any unprofitable relationship, in the name of Jesus.
9. I break every ungodly relationship, in the name of Jesus.
10. I break and renounce evil soul ties I have had with homosexuals, fornicators, adulterers, former husband, former wife, doctors, nurses, past or present friends, cults members, societal club members, lecturers, teachers, and evil friends.

11. I renounce all hidden evil soul ties, in the name of Jesus.
12. Let evil affections toward me be wiped off the mind of *(Mention the name)* in the name of Jesus.
13. You, the spirit and power behind homosexual act in my life, release me and let me go, in the name of Jesus.
14. You, the spirit and power behind (mention the kind of sexual perversion you find yourself in; it could be masturbation, lesbianism) et cetera, loose me and let me go, in the name of Jesus.
15. I break myself loose from every spirit of sexual perversion.
16. I release myself from every spiritual pollution emanating from my past sexual sins of fornication and other sexual immoralities.
17. I command every evil plantation of sexual perversions in my life to be uprooted, in the name of Jesus.
18. Every demon of sexual perversions in my life, be bound, in the name of Jesus.
19. Let the power of sexual perversions oppressing my life receive fire of God and be roasted.
20. You power of sexual perversions that have consumed my life, be shattered, in the name of Jesus.
21. Oh God of Elijah! Arise with your strong hand against every spirit wife and power of sexual perversion operating in my life, in the name of Jesus.

22. I claim my total deliverance from every spirit of fornication or adultery, or any form of sexual immorality.
23. Holy Ghost fire! Fall upon my eyes and burn to ashes every evil force and other satanic power controlling my eyes, in Jesus name.
24. I move from bondage to liberty in every area of my life, in the name of Jesus.
25. Thank the Lord for all the answered prayers.

ABOUT THE AUTHOR

Samuel Kunle-Oluwatobi is a Graphic Designer and Artist from Lagos, Nigeria. He holds a master's degree in communication and language arts from the University of Ibadan, Nigeria, having previously studied graphic design at Yaba College of Technology, Yaba Lagos. He trained as a minister under Dr. D. K. Olukoya, and has pioneered (pastored) different branches of Mountain Fire and Miracles Ministries at different times.

Samuel Kunle-Oluwatobi is a member of many advertising professional associations among which are: Advertising Practitioners Council of Nigeria (APCON), The Certified Marketing Communications Institute of Nigeria (CMCIN), International Association of Business Communicators (IABC), Nigeria Institute of Public Relations NIPR, and is also an affiliate member of Chartered Institute of Public Relations CIPR, UK. He is a Creative and Corporate Communications Consultant and the Shepherd of Sam Kunle-Oluwatobi Ministries—a Word of God and power-based evangelical outfit committed to winning souls for Christ.

Samuel Kunle-Oluwatobi has authored other books which include: Power of Sex, Teens Sexuality Guide—10 Rules for Purity Till Marriage, Choose Your Spouse Wisely—Using 21 Rules from Biblical Principles as Searchlight, and other coming books: Civics for making Civilized People—Social Responsibility Rules, Know Your Rights and Obligations as a Citizen, Your Rights as a Wife under Marital Covenant, and Ten Living Ethics of Marriage.

Kunle-Oluwatobi is an anointed teacher, pastor, and evangelist with a very strong prophetic ministry. He ministers the words of God and the gospel of Jesus Christ to the world through his preaching, teaching, and writing. He is presently based in Lagos, Nigeria.

For further Information
Please visit:
samkunle-oluwatobiministries.com
Or
Send e-mail to:
samuel.kunleoluwatobi@yahoo.com
kunleoluwatobisamuel@gmail.com
Tel: +234-803-7137-741,
      +234-807-2565-389.

And please follow the Author Sam Kunle-Oluwatobi on Twitter, facebook, linkedIn, pininterest, Google+, netlog, etc

Made in the USA
Monee, IL
03 May 2026